Meandering

Notes of a Mississippi Riverlorian

T0159599

Meandering

Notes of a Mississippi Riverlorian

By
Mike Link
&
Kate Crowley

NORTH STAR PRESS OF ST. CLOUD, INC.
St. Cloud, Minnesota

ISBN: 978-0-87839-806-5

First edition: May 2016

Printed in the United States of America.

Published by
North Star Press of St. Cloud, Inc.
P.O. Box 451
St. Cloud, MN 56302

www.northstarpress.com

Table of Contents

Introduction

Following the Meanders

From walking around Lake Superior to exploring the Mississippi River, the last five years have been a focus on freshwater resources, trying to learn about their complexity and sharing their importance. In *Going Full Circle* we documented our hike around Lake Superior, and we hoped to do something similar with the Mississippi River, but as we began to explore and learn, we could not find a simple way to capture the diverse stories of this 2,350-mile-long river. We began to use a variety of ways to try and capture a sense of place.

Our narrative reflects on the river and its roots in ecology and geography, but we also had to explore culture, geography, and the diversity along this longitudinal corridor, which is amazing. These are the building blocks for the stories in this meandering narrative.

Leading a hike in Baton Rouge, one of the people in the group said, "Meandering with Mike, we never know where we will go," and that stuck for the title. This story combines past adventures with current explorations. But like the river itself, the story meanders; it runs up against an obstacle and turns, it floods with information and flows out of the usual banks that control a writer's path. This book is an exploration with strange details popping up at unexpected places.

Our journey by bike, hike, and boat began by car and so it follows a logical path by road from beginning to end, but then we switched to the water in both exploring and writing. We realized the futility of seeing the river from the road and from beyond the levees or crossing on bridges. We were able to touch the people and places that surrounded the river, but not the essence of the Mississippi itself. Our narrative will follow downstream from place to place in logical geographic order, but the dates and times are not sequential.

In the Lower Mississippi, we hope to create the final picture of the southern river, and we have to say that we not only did the south first, we went upstream in the south and downstream in the north—meeting our perspectives in the Middle Mississippi, where the Gateway Arch pulls together all the directions and stories. Returning to many sections multiple times, we have now traveled 8,812 miles on the river since 2011 (and over 1,500 canoe miles in previous years). We did this in multiple months and seasons, avoiding frozen lakes and flooding rivers. We saw all the seasons and tried to find the variety. In addition, we have driven 7,840 miles of river length, walked 566 miles, and biked 1,000 miles. And we will be covering more miles as the book is read.

As the book will explain, we have been on the upper thousand miles of the river many times with many groups, but this river is never the same. The cliché about not being able to step in the same river twice, referring to the fact that the water does not stand still and, therefore, each time one enter, one encounters new water, is compounded by the continually changing weather and the flow of commerce and people. Ours is a story we can dip our minds into, but it will change every time we go back.

This is also a continuation of our concern for fresh water—our most precious of all resources. There is a cavalier approach to water that scares us. Whether it is the fracking of our ground waters, the intrusive and careless construction of pipelines, or the farm chemicals, road and municipal wastes, and the pollution of Cancer Alley (the concentration of petrochemical corporations between Baton Rouge and New Orleans), the water we see going in to the Gulf is water no one would want to drink. Fish continue to live there, though in smaller populations, and people are warned not to eat them. We produce chemical fertilizers and pesticides as products of the petroleum processing, ship them north to be put on the land in our agricultural and urban locations in excess of what is needed, and they return south in the water, back to their place of origin and finally into the Gulf, where we have created a massive deadzone—a lifeless area as big as New Jersey where much of the petroleum is being drilled and piped or shipped back to Cancer Alley. We are replacing natural cycles with human-dominated cycles and somewhere, somehow, we have to go back to what is really important—water to drink, air to breathe, and non-toxic food to eat.

Chapter One

The Mississippi

MIKE

Oᴜʀ ᴄᴏɴɴᴇᴄᴛɪᴏɴ to the Mississippi could be traced to many sources. It could have been because Kate and I grew up in Minneapolis, she near Minnehaha Creek, the famous tributary that plunges over one of the most famous waterfalls in Minnesota before joining the river, and me in a variety of neighborhoods, none on a tributary, but always near enough to make the Mississippi part of my childhood memories. I remember the days of playing in Riverside Park across from the main campus of the University of Minnesota, crawling around on the limestone rocks and running between the trees.

As we grew up, the cityscape also grew with us. The river became part of the Grand Round, the old buildings and bridges became parkways and tourist attractions. I paddled the river and its tributaries, biked and walked its parkways and considered the river to be part of my neighborhood, no matter where I lived in the city. Kate continued to live near the creek and saw her son, Jon, play in and enjoy it as he developed his love of nature and adventure.

My love of nature began with a canoe trip on the Rum River, and it fostered a desire to float on every blue line that marked the state maps of Minnesota and Wisconsin. This, of course, led me to the Mississippi. There are 7,000 rivers that empty into the Mississippi, and who knows how many hundreds of thousands of rivulets empty into these tributaries.

Any of these facts could have been our driving force, but they were not.

Our exploration of the Mississippi River began on September 18, 2010, when we completed our walk around Lake Superior. Our *Going Full Circle* adventure was winding down, but our concern for fresh water was strengthened and my personal desire for another adventure was already being kindled. As I hobbled the last few miles to the end of the walk, I was already sorry to see our trip end. I wanted more. It was that desire that made me think about our commitment to fresh water and how we could continue to build on the desire to make people think about irreplaceable resource.

As an ecologist and college instructor, I worked with teachers to better understand water. I wanted them to pass their knowledge on to their students. Like the flow of the rivers, my knowledge passed to the teachers, the teachers to the students, and hopefully from there to action, concern, and protection of the resources.

Minnesota bills itself as the "Land of 10,000 Lakes," an interesting understatement. I explain to people from other states that this is the Minnesotan attitude Garrison Keillor plays off on *A Prairie Home Companion*—an understated people not prone to bragging. As a consequence, we round down instead of up when we use the 10,000 figure. It indicates a lot of water, but not all of it.

The Minnesota Department of Natural Resources (DNR) lists 11,842 lakes over ten acres in size, and out of eighty-seven counties in the state, only Mower, Olmsted, Pipestone, and Rock have no lakes. They do have rivers and wetlands, however. Wetlands have diminished from 18.6 million acres in 1850 to 10.62 million in 2012, according to the Minnesota DNR, which is a loss for everyone but still represents a large freshwater resource. According to the same DNR web source, there are 6,564 natural rivers and streams (the difference between a river, creek, and stream is something no one can really answer) with 69,200 miles of flow within the state.

One river, the St. Louis, is the westernmost flow into Lake Superior, and as a result we think of it as the headwaters to the entire Great Lakes System. It is also the water that forms the Duluth/Superior harbor, which is often mistaken for a portion of the lake. The St. Louis comes out of the famous Boundary Waters Canoe Area Wilderness (BWCAW), another major Minnesota water resource with world renown. According to the early writings of Warren Upham, the Ojibwe name of the river is Gichigami-ziibi (Great-lake River), which feels like a confirmation of our assumption. Unfortunately, the name of a French king was put on the river by Verendrye (this is not confirmed, but considered likely) and the better name was lost to history.

The St. Louis flows 192 miles, starts near the town of Hoyt Lakes, and is easily canoed for a long stretch. As is curves around to make its run toward the harbor, it flows within Jay Cooke State Park. The Grand Portage used by voyageurs to travel up the river and past the complex and dangerous rapids bypassed the one-mile, one-hundred-foot drop featured in the park. Yes, there is a Grand Portage that is famous on Lake Superior near the Canadian border, but that name was a description of a long carry and not intended as an official place name, such as it is now. This Grand Portage—which we have hiked—is slippery red clay when wet and steep with ravines of bedrock and clay.

The voyageurs slogged through tough terrain to get back on the river and upstream to the Savanna Portage, seventy-two miles from Lake Superior and now marked by a Minnesota State Park. Irving Hart wrote,

> In the northeastern part of Aitkin County, Minnesota, lie two small lakes, Savanne [sic] and Wolf, distinguished in no way from thousands of other lakes which make this part of the country a paradise for hunter, fisherman, and tourist; but significant beyond all others because of the physiographic fact that here the waters of the Mississippi

and the St. Lawrence [Great Lakes] systems approach each other more closely than at any other place in Minnesota. It was this fact which rendered it inevitable, in the days when transportation was largely by canoe and portage, that this particular region should become the site of one of the most important portage routes in the Northwest.

The portage connected the Savannah River to the Mississippi River. The land connection between the two is just six miles long—but what a six miles! This is not up and over like the earlier grand portage; this is flat, wet, and thick swamp. The best description might be from the 1820 Lewis Cass (who was the governor of Midiigan—later renamed Michigan—territory) expedition from Detroit to the Mississippi. Doctor Alexander Wolcott left this description in his journal:

> The length of the Savannah portage is six miles, and is passed at thirteen pauses. The first three pauses are shockingly bad. It is not only a bed of mire, but the difficulty of passing it is greatly increased by fallen trees, limbs, and sharp knots of the pitch pine, in some places on the surface, in others imbedded one or two feet below. Where there are hollows or depressions in the ground, tall coarse grass, brush, and pools of stagnant water are encountered. Old voyageurs say that this part of the portage was formerly covered with a heavy bog, or a kind of peat, upon which the walking was very good, but that during a dry season, it accidentally caught fire and burnt over the surface of the earth so as to lower its level two or three feet when it became mirey, and subject to inundation from the Savannah river. The country, after passing the third pause, changes in a short distance, from a marsh to a region of sand hills covered mostly with white and yellow pine, intermixed with aspen. The hills are short and conical, with a moderate elevation. In some places they are drawn into ridges, but these ridges cannot be observed to run in any uniform course. . . . Where the portage approaches the sources of the West Savannah there is a descent into a small valley covered with rank grass—without forest trees—and here and there clumps of willows. . . . The valley is skirted with a thick and brushy growth of alder, aspen, hazel, &c. The adjoining hills are sandy, covered with pine. The stream here is just large enough to swim a canoe, and the navigation commences within a mile of its source. It pursues a very serpentine course to Sandy Lake . . . a distance of six miles.

The Great Lakes are separated from the Great River by six miles! The Great River (Mississippi) collects the waters from thirty-one states and two Canadian provinces on its 2,350-mile course from Lake Itasca to the Gulf of Mexico, and was the inspiration for numerous explorations to discover its source. Famous explorers like LaSalle, DeSoto, Joliet, Radisson, Hennepin, Marquette, Nicollet, Zebulon Pike, and finally Schoolcraft labored to discover what the Native Americans already knew—they had a village at Itasca. The challenge of naming the source was a powerful inspiration for the explorers.

Now a state park, Itasca, sits on the lake that is the agreed-upon source (some have wanted to consider Elk Lake and its little outflow to Itasca to be the source, but to settle the controversy the Minnesota government passed a law that made Itasca the final word). It is an inspiring place with forests of large, old-growth red and white pines and a picturesque beginning to the river that reflects our human influence—originally the river just ran out of the boggy landscape at the north end of the lake, but rocks were put in place and a channel designated to become the official start. Millions have walked these rocks thinking that it is a natural spot and loving the idea of stepping in the water as it leaves for its rendezvous with the Gulf of Mexico.

With this geographic landscape in mind we began to think of Minnesota as a distributary—a place which outsources its water to the Great Lakes and the Gulf, and in fact to Hudson Bay and the Arctic through the northern flow of the Red River on the Minnesota and South Dakota/North Dakota borders. We receive it in pure form and then it begins to move on, but what happens as it moves is the problem.

Rivers have been thought of as places to get rid of waste—all kinds of waste—because the water naturally takes the materials downstream. People feel good if they live upstream, but more people live downstream than at the source and nature has only a limited amount of resources to clean up the pesticides, herbicides, fertilizers, lawn and road runoff, petroleum products, and invasive species, in its natural channel. Living downstream is dangerous and the impact of thoughtless use of water is something we have to come to terms with.

On our hike around Lake Superior, we shared the message that two things are most essential to life—clean air and clean water—and there is no room for compromise. Both must be treated as the precious commodities they truly are.

From Full Circle to Full Length, we decided to carry our message and hope to create a positive forum for people to think about their legacy, to care about future generations and to leave the two most precious commodities in the healthy state required for life. But we did not know at that time that BP's Deepwater Horizon spill would add a complex and terrible message to our journeys.

Chapter Two

The River

MIKE

Disclaimer: Okay, this is about geology and science! Legos did not put this river together; a complex system of landforms, continental glaciers, the erosive action of water, and the broad scope of geography make up this fascinating system. This is the simple version of the recipe book that has taken millions of years to become what we see today. It is a recipe that cannot be replicated, which is why it is so important to understand it and preserve the most significant watershed on the continent.

Since we walked around the largest lake in the world by surface area, Lake Superior, much of what we do is in comparison. Lake Superior is 31,700 square miles—1,555 miles around—with a watershed of 49,300 square miles and 1,934 rivers which empty into it. The Mississippi River is 2,350 miles long with an average one-mile width—2,350 square miles with a watershed of 1,200,000 square miles and 7,000 rivers including such giants as the Missouri, Ohio, Wisconsin, Minnesota, Illinois, and Red emptying in. That is the difference between a small and a gigantic watershed.

What Is the Mississippi?

How to describe the Mississippi? It is called the Great River, a translation of a native term, but that does not seem adequate. Hamline's Center for Global Environmental Education states, "The Ojibway Indians of northern Minnesota called it 'Messipi' or 'Big River,' and it was also known as the 'Mee-zee-see-bee' or the 'Father of Waters.'" European explorers who mapped all the river's channels and backwater areas called it a "gathering of waters." The Missouri/Mississippi combined flow is greater than that which is designated the Mississippi River. In fact, numerous options lay before the discoverers of the Mississippi source—they could have turned

up larger rivers, including the very large Ohio and Missouri, each of which might have had more water flowing in them than the river that came from the north, but the route north just felt right. A great river should begin in the north—not the east (Ohio) or west (Missouri)—so the adventurers, from de Soto to Marquette, to Pike, to Schoolcraft, kept moving to the northern wilds of what would become Minnesota—the North Star State.

On a map, the waterway designated as the Mississippi has been described as a fishhook, but even though that seems appropriate for a watery environment, I prefer to think of it as a question mark. Its charm for so many explorers was that it came from some unknown place in the north. It could have been in Canada, or it could have been the Minnesota River, which flows out of the valley of the ancient River Warren, but the Minnesota, like the previous options, did not come from the north.

Time for a disclaimer—there is no resemblance between the current Minnesota River and the historic flow called the River Warren. The River Warren took the outflow of Lake Agassiz and carved an amazingly deep and wide valley in a very short time, but a good valley should not be wasted and so the Min-

nesota River occupied this outsized valley. The river followed the margin of a glacial moraine (a theme that will continue over and over in the Upper Mississippi), swung southeast and then northeast before turning south again and moving through the driftless area of Minnesota, Wisconsin, Iowa, and Illinois.

The driftless (unglaciated) area is at the corner of four states the glacier did not cover. Various factors account for this, including the fingers (lobes) that were diverted at the front of the massive continental glacier. Some moved fast, some slow. They were diverted by old river valleys (Lake Superior today) or followed others like Lake Michigan and kept moving rapidly in one direction. These errant lobes went in many directions and may, in fact, have had a traffic jam where all the members budged up against one another. The result was this island, sometimes referred to as a refugia, where plants and animals could continue to exist if they could stand the refrigerated conditions.

Today we think of the driftless zone as a deep, bluff-lined valley of the Mississippi, but the Mississippi never had the volume and force needed to make this valley. It was the River Warren that did the heavy lifting, or rather the heavy excavating. I cannot imagine the impact of that water getting all the way to the Gulf of Mexico, but it got there! The Mississippi took the path of least resistance, and once it reached what is now the Twin Cities, it followed the newly excavated River Warren valley.

Explorers continued to find smaller and smaller waterways attached to the larger stream. Even when they eventually reached the northern lakes, they kept looking for more extensions of the stream. Pike quit at Leech Lake, which today is joined to the Mississippi by the Leech River, and others quit at other lakes, but the lure to find the final source caused the explorers to seek more waters as they moved west through Winnibigoshish, Cass Lake, Lake Bemidji, and Irving. The explorers continued seeking another northern source flow, but more importantly, wanted to find a source no one else had claimed. After Lake Bemidji, near the Northernmost point on the Mississippi, explorers and mapmakers were forced to look south to the beginning of the "?" and finally came to Lake Itasca.

The Indian agent Schoolcraft was the discoverer of the source according to history, but the tribe that lived along the stream and lake might have wondered at this fact. And of course, even after Schoolcraft others wanted to claim Elk Lake and Nicollet Lake and their flows into Itasca as the

source. This might have been done except that the state legislature stepped in and made these claims invalid, setting Schoolcraft's designation as the law of the land. In other words, the Mississippi River is constructed of a variety of streams, none more logically Mississippi than the others along the route. The rivulets, creeks, streams, rivers, and flows that were finally cobbled together to create the Mississippi only became the true river because someone said so, and now it is on a map and in a law.

The Mississippi River Ancestry

THE MISSISSIPPI RIVER we know today is not ancient in geologic history. It was not providing liquid to the dinosaur, but the southern end may have given liquid satisfaction for the great mammoths and mastodons. For much of geologic history the Mississippi River valley was underwater—under an ocean. The land we explore today was built up by deposition of oceanic sandstones and limestone, the accumulation of fossiliferous organisms, and a variety of near shore deposits, with the exception of the Ozark Plateau in southern Missouri and Illinois.

This highland is sometimes called the Ozark Mountains. In Illinois, it is also called the Shawnee Hills, and some geologists and geographers describe it as a separate formation. The plateau is also called a dome and has formed around the Saint Francois Mountains of southeastern Missouri. Important to this story is the fact that these "Interior Highlands," as the Ouachita, Boston, Saint Francois, and Ozarks are collectively called, combine both limestone that gives us springs and caves as well as a highly dissected plateau and some volcanic rocks in the Saint Francois portion. Granitic and rhyolitic rocks dating from 1,485 to 1,350 million years ago with fringing reefs add diversity to the flat layers of sediment that are exposed from the Twin Cities to the Gulf.

Tributaries from this high country include some of the most spectacular wild and scenic rivers in the National Park System—the Jack's Fork, Current, and Buffalo. The natural spring waters that circulate through the limestone keep these waters cold and clear until they merge with the Big Muddy. Having paddled all these rivers, I can tell you that the color of the water was the most striking feature—a blue-green clear water emanating from underground springs that is both refreshing and beautiful.

At its source, the Mississippi River owes its origin story to continental glaciers, specifically the Wisconsin Glaciation. At the headwaters the elevation of the river is 1,475 feet and, of course, it ends in the Gulf of Mexico at sea level: zero feet. The Great Ice Age is the source for the Great Lakes and the Great River, the paths of the Missouri and Ohio River, as well as the great flow of water in Glacial River Warren that dug the deep valley through the driftless (unglaciated) highlands of Iowa, Minnesota, Wisconsin, and Illinois.

Think of Everest Buried in Ice and Snow

THE TRUE SOURCE of the Mississippi, Ohio, Missouri, Wisconsin and many more of our great watershed rivers is found in glacial moraine complexes. Moraines are hill systems that build up during the melting of the glaciers—a time when the movement and the melt are equal. With new ice replacing that which has melted, the glacier becomes a conveyor moving the eroded rocks it has accumulated along its path to the leading edge of the fingers of ice that glaciologists call lobes. The build-up of a deep deposit of debris, rocks, boulders, and ice blocks discarded by the melt forms gentle ridges of hills that cover hundreds of miles from Montana to Pennsylvania.

Within these hilly regions were large sections of ice that became incorporated in the glacial discard and preserved for decades by the insulating overburden. As the ice age ended, the sun's warmth was absorbed by the stones and sediments. The initial meltwater would disperse, leaving a hole or kettle. If water draining to and from the hole brought enough silt and clay to fill the holes between rocks and sediments, the kettle would refill with rain and snow—giving us our modern land of lakes.

Let's take a time out to understand. Geologists use some terms that most people are not comfortable with, words that are not part of everyday vocabulary. To start with, what is continental glaciation? Without discussing the causes, we know a pulse has gone on for billions of years on earth where ice and snow accumulate to great depths in the northern continents. Less so in the southern continents, with the exception of Antarctica, because South America, Australia, and Africa do not extend to the Antarctic Circle like the land mass in Europe, Asia, and North America overlap the Arctic Circle.

The ice ages were not a winter; they were millennia of ice and snow that built up to depths of three to five miles—deep enough to bury Mount Everest. The ice was so thick and heavy the continental mass squeezed the Earth's mantle. The ice moved and nothing could stop it. It occasionally ran into hot periods, especially as it moved south, where the margins melted back, only to be reinvigorated by the cold in the north. This lively edge of the glacier was not square—not a giant ice cube. Instead, the margins broke into finger-like projections called lobes, and the lobes worked like fingers of a potter to shape the landscape in different ways along each front.

As one might imagine, when every square foot of land is subjected to the pressure equivalent of 150 cars stacked upon themselves, the rocks are going to give. The freezing and thawing is going to weaken the rock. Think of a snail or clam moving on its feeding foot (lobe) taking in and ingesting materials as it moves—that is how the rocks get into the glacier. But the scale soon makes the snail analogy too difficult.

What is important is the fact that the glacial lobes become more than ice and snow—there are rocks and boulders, sediments, and even some organic matter that travels with the ice and eventually falls out where it thaws. Nothing truly stops a glacier, it just melts. The accumulation of materials from the ice are increased when the glacier moves quicker than it melts, they are distributed in great concentrations when movement and melt are equal, and are randomly distributed if the glacier melts faster than it moves.

Besides creating moraines, the melting of the ice creates a great abundance of water, and the freshly configured landscape does not have a system of rivers and drainage in place. Large temporary lakes (temporary may mean a few hundred years) dot the countryside. But when the earthen dams of glacial deposits break, the water is released to become a moving and erosive force. When the Thompson Dam near Rocky Mountain National Park broke, the resulting wall of water wiped out towns and highways, but was nothing when compared to the power of rivers suddenly draining large glacial lakes and valleys.

Back to the Mississippi

THE CURRENT STREAM rolls north from its source, flowing off the backside of the moraine toward Canada. It meanders from Itasca State Park to Lake Bemidji and in and out of moraine lakes. Irving, Wolf, Andalusia, Bemidji, Cass, Winnibigoshish, and little Winny are not the only lakes in the moraine, but during the evolution of the river, each of their drainages were pirated (captured by the movement of the waters out of Itasca). Each time a stream was captured, the flow of the young Mississippi intensified its erosion. This repeated combination of events put the current hook in the Mississippi River, a stream assembled like a Tinker Toy rather than a roaring river.

The random pattern of little streams and big lakes creates the crescent or top of the question mark/hook. The water leaves the south side of the moraine and descends down to the lower glacial plain.

Near the town of Aitkin, Minnesota, the stream entered a temporary glacial lake that had been impounded by glacial debris. This was Glacial Lake Aitkin, and its flat lake bottom slowed the Mississippi River's current, resulting in meanders. Meanders are a result of the stream being unable to move its flow at the normal speed. The resistance backs up the river. To release this pent-up energy, the river elongates and spreads the energy through a series of twists and turns.

The river rolled across a soggy landscape shiny with water and ice. Fish moved up into this drainage from the south, plants came on the feet of migrating birds, and seeds were carried by the fresh winds off the glacier while warmer breezes blew in from the south. Some plant seeds had been preserved by the big glacial ice cooler. Lichens appeared on the rocks, followed by mosses and flowers and shrubs and trees. Mammals tested the northern landscape and moved slowly to fill the new habitats while the woodland Native Americans found places to live, resources to support life, and adapted to a changing world.

The river edges down through St. Cloud, Monticello, Elk River, and the Twin Cities, growing tributary by tributary as it moves toward St. Anthony Falls, the only waterfall on the river. Today, the combination of Nicollet Island, the lock and dams, and Spirit Island has become the gateway to the Twin Cities canyon.

The Big Valley

AT RIVER MILE 845, the Minnesota River (322 miles) joins the Mississippi. The Minnesota is the river of Eric Severeid's great adventure, where he and another friend canoed to Lake Winnipeg as told in the classic book *Canoeing with the Cree*. The Minnesota River starts on the South Dakota border in the same lake that flows north as the Red River. The Red flows slowly through the old Lake Agassiz bed. Agassiz was the largest freshwater lake in the planet's history and covered all of northwest Minnesota, parts of North Dakota, and a lot of the Canadian provinces of Manitoba, Saskatchewan, and Ontario. When it drained, it eroded its small glacial dam and erupted with such force that it formed the huge Minnesota River valley.

Not far from the Minnesota/Mississippi convergence, another option arose for the early explorers to choose the path of the Mississippi. This one actually comes from the north at river mile 810—the St. Croix River (169 miles). What we now consider to be a tributary was another result of glacial great lakes, or in this case, two lakes: Lake Duluth in Minnesota and Lake Grantsburg in Wisconsin.

First the waters of Lake Duluth, 500 feet above the current lake level, washed down the Brule and St Croix valleys—the two rivers now flow opposite directions from Lake St Croix, but at that time they both flowed south—and they emptied into Glacial Lake Grantsburg. Lake Grantsburg was a long east-west lake, and the energy of its outflow can be seen at Taylor's Falls on the Minnesota and Wisconsin border, where the rivers carved the dells of Interstate Park through ancient volcanic rocks. Where the Mississippi and St Croix join, the river floodplain is one to three miles wide.

Lake Pepin is the last natural lake on the Mississippi and is a result of the Chippewa River and its massive sediment load. The Chippewa River (mile 765—153 miles long) flows from the lakes and highlands of northeastern Wisconsin. On its diagonal trip across a large part of northern Wisconsin, the river gathers both the water and the sediments from numerous tributary streams. Sediment is a part of all rivers. Still water allows the sediment to settle. Lakes will accumulate clay because they are still, but the lightness of clay means it stays suspended in moving water. Silt is the next size of sediment, and it too stays suspended until the waters move up and out of the banks of the river during floods. The flood plain slows the water and increases the sedimentation, so silt is accumulated here.

Sand is much larger than the silt and clay and requires a relatively fast current to continue downstream. When a river enters a lake or the

ocean, it slows down and loses the energy to move sand. The result is sandy deltas and beaches. When the Chippewa enters the Mississippi, the big Miss is so large that the Chippewa loses strength and the sand that has traveled down its course is accumulated. The year I paddled the Chippewa, I was fascinated by the sand patterns on the river bottom as we approached the Mississippi. In the lowest stretches the slowing down process is already in evidence, and the sand will sit until floodwaters scour it out and push it toward the big river. This sediment will be forced into the bigger river, but it will not be moved downstream. Instead, the delta will be crisscrossed by the two streams and cut into the islands beneath Lake Pepin.

The sand enters and creates barrier spits, islands, and filled channels, and generally slows the big Mississippi to almost a standstill. The Chippewa waters and sediments are a living dam, and the lake is a natural reservoir. The wide Pepin flow cannot make it through the reduced channel, and consequently Lake City and its Wisconsin counterparts are located on a forty-square-mile river/lake.

I am partial to the Chippewa because it is also the river that my great-great grandfather John Quaderer eventually journeyed up after landing in New Orleans in 1850. Ancestry.com says,

> He immigrated to America in 1852 and landed at New Orleans, Louisiana. Coming to Wisconsin by way of Chicago in June of that year, he worked on a farm in Dodge County for one year, and then engaged as river driver on the Mississippi river for one season. He then went to Dubuque, Iowa, and engaged with Knapp, Stout & Co. in the lumber yards at that point. He was sent to Menomonie by them and then, in 1854, up the river to Barron County, as a cutter of pine timber.

He founded the town of Barron, Wisconsin, but his loggers continued to send their logs down the Red Cedar and Chippewa rivers to the Mississippi. While the sand settled, the logs moved on.

As the rivers roll down from the highlands of the driftless area they have the energy of a quick elevation change and the river is studded with outflow deltas. The Zumbro enters at mile 760 (sixty-four miles long) from Minnesota and deposits its sand in a delta that includes the locally famous sand dunes. This is where the natural area called Weaver Bottoms can be found. Wabasha, with the National Eagle Center, anchors the northern "top" of the delta, while Maloney Lake forms a wonderful wetland shallows for the Upper Mississippi River National Wildlife Refuge at the southern end.

The refuge is one of the most important waterfowl areas in the Midwest, providing habitat for 125 fish species and thirty species of freshwater mussels. We love to explore by canoe during warbler migration—it is not just ducks that benefit from the wetlands and dissected deltas of the Buffalo, Trempealeau, and Black rivers in Wisconsin. There is a mix of islands and waterways where waterfowl nest and furbearers like mink and otter prosper. The richness there is a northern equivalent of the Atchafalaya River in Louisiana.

The La Crosse River (mile 698—sixty-one miles long) comes in by its namesake city, while on the Minnesota shores the Root River establishes wetlands. When the Upper Iowa River becomes part of the Mississippi (mile 671), we have reached the far northeast corner of the state of Iowa. This river differs from the Minnesota and Wisconsin rivers in that it is not of glacial origin. On a five-day river trip along the Upper Iowa years ago, we canoed through delicate limestone features called chimneys and under massive limestone cliffs. These would have been destroyed by the glaciers or even massive river runoff like the River Warren. It was a river with fossils mixed in the limestone gravel and steep limestone bluffs along its course.

I remember it because my partner at the time, Mick Sommer, and I were young and foolish. We ate burgers and salad three times a day. Then near the mouth we walked up a steep grade to look for rattlesnakes on the limestone rocks. We did not find any, but coming down the steep grade Mick woke one sleeping in the warm leaf litter. As I followed in his steps, the snake reacted to the second person in line. Raising its head and shaking the rattle, he sent me leaping into space and tumbling down the hillside. The driftless area is the home to timber rattlesnakes on the bluffs and massasauga, another species of rattlesnake, in the river bottoms.

The next major river from the east is the Rock River (mile 479), a 199-mile river that begins in the glacial landscape of northern Wisconsin and flows southwest through Illinois to join the Mississippi River at Rock Island/Moline, Illinois. Rock Island is where Ronald Reagan served as a lifeguard in his youth in Dixon, and he fished at a place now called Dutch Landing. The island is now the largest in the Mississippi River. One reference claimed it was once part of a waterfall that would have rivaled

Niagara. Before the locks and dams and alterations in the substrate, this was a serious rock rapids.

Traveling in the same southwestern direction as the Chippewa, Wisconsin, and Rock rivers, the Illinois River cuts a swath across the state from Chicago to a point just north of Alton. The Illinois (mile 219—273 miles) has long been a source of boating, from the Native populations to the fishermen of today, but it is the commercial use of the river that has caused conflict in recent years. Due to the construction of the Illinois and Michigan Canal and the Hennepin Canal in the nineteenth century, the waterway now connects the Mississippi River with Lake Michigan. In Chicago, the city fathers reversed the flow of the Chicago River and have created a pathway for commerce to move to the Gulf. The conflict raging today for all Great Lakes enthusiasts is the fact that the Illinois River is infested with Asian carp, and the spread of the carp to the Great Lakes is most probable through this combination of river and canals. The invasive fish has already spread to the Mississippi River and has been breeding there since the 1970s. These fish were imported by fish farmers in southern states to help clean commercial ponds, and at least one source said they escaped during flood waters.

Both invasive silver and bighead carp are called Asian carp. They are voracious eaters and consume the same food our native sport fish require. The carp can reach over 100 pounds and our native species cannot compete. They are considered to be skittish fish, and when startled by motors, they can leap into the air (as much as ten feet out of the water) and land on boats or even knock people out of them—think of a flying 100-pound torpedo rising out of the water.

Tributaries As Big As or Bigger Than the Mississippi
THE UPPER MISSISSIPPI ends with two big tributaries, the Missouri and the Ohio. I cannot begin to imagine how the explorers could have bypassed them and said the little guy from the north was the true Mississippi, but lucky for Minnesota, that was the case.

The Missouri (mile 196) is best known as the river of Louis and Clark, but of course it is much more than that. This was the gateway to the west, the reason St. Louis existed. From here the fur traders would journey down from the Rocky Mountain rendezvous to sell their skins. It was where

commerce intersected and the continent was connected, long before any arch was contemplated. Here the Trail of Tears and the Underground Railroad intersect with the Lewis and Clark Expedition, the steamboats, the railroads, stagecoach trails, continental railroads, and the highways.

The Missouri River wends its way through the Great Plains, where it erodes soft rocks and picks up the silt and mud that give both it and the lower Mississippi the name "Big Muddy."

The Mississippi/Missouri/Jefferson River is the third longest river in the world at 3,902 miles (6,275 kilometers). Alone, the designated Mississippi only makes it into the top forty—a great river, but not quite as great as its name and reputation. To world geographers, the Missouri and the Mississippi constitute one river. The Missouri by itself is the longest river in North America, stretching 2,341 miles long before it enters the Mississippi, and if we designated one of the three rivers (the Madison River) that combine to make the Missouri, as the explorers did for the Mississippi, we would add another 183 miles. The river drops 8,626 feet in its journey, compared to the 1,430 feet the Mississippi drops from Itasca to the Gulf.

Like the Mississippi, the course and the shape of the mighty Missouri River must be traced to the glaciers. Prior to the last big ice age advance, the streams at the source of the Missouri (Madison, Jefferson, and Gallatin) flowed north, and like the Mississippi River, the initial phase of the river still does. But the ice sheet blocked the northern drainage and dammed the waters, creating both lakes and a barrier. The waters had no place to go but through this system of lakes and flow along the edge of the glacier. Glaciation, as we noted earlier, was not uniform and as the river moved through Montana into the Dakotas, the lobes extended further south, curving the river system. The result was the great crescent we see when we look at the river on a map. It is also interesting to note that the Missouri's major tributaries come from the south

and the west. Had the glaciers not appeared, the Missouri River would have still flowed, but instead of being part of the Mississippi/Missouri River flowing to the Gulf, the waters would have moved north to the Arctic Ocean and Lewis and Clark would have had a much harder journey.

From the Missouri to the Ohio River is the unofficial middle Mississippi. The upper Mississippi, according to the Army Corp of Engineers, goes until Cairo, Illinois, and the confluence with the Ohio River.

The Ohio is the third of the three big arms of the watershed flowing east to west beneath the great lakes. This was the river of Johnny Appleseed, numerous western pioneers, and the great naturalist James J. Audubon. Combined with the Missouri, it fueled the dreams of the Northwest Passage to the Pacific. In fact, the Ohio has the most waterflow of the three major rivers that combine to form the lower Mississippi.

The story of the Ohio has to do with the eastern ice lobes of the continental glacier. The eastern rivers once drained into the Lake Erie region, but the ice blocked all northern flows and concentrated the waters along

the margin of glacial deposit, forming massive lakes that helped force the development of the river. If you combine the distance of both the Missouri and Ohio rivers, there was an ice face 3,850 miles long that melted and drained like a funnel into the lower Mississippi.

Southern Mississippi River Tributaries—the Lower Mississippi

AFTER THE OHIO RIVER, the White River National Wildlife Refuge in Arkansas drains the flow of the Buffalo, Jack's Fork, and Current National Wild and Scenic rivers. Next are the Arkansas and Big Black river (used by Grant in the overall battle strategy to capture Vicksburg) and the Yazoo.

The Yazoo River joins the Mississippi at Vicksburg. The Yazoo and the Mississippi converge after miles of a parallel course that has created the famous Delta country of Mississippi cotton and blues fame. The Yazoo was named by LaSalle in 1682 for the Indians who lived in the area—"Riviere des Yazous."

Downstream, there are no dams and locks to control the river. Instead, there are levees. From 1858 to 1927 there were twelve major floods, with 1927 the worst. John Barry writes a moving narrative of this

region in his book *Rising Tide*, a very sad story of death, racism, and the destruction of towns and homes. Over 162,000 homes were flooded and the devastation was responsible for many of the federal efforts and agencies that continue today. After 1927, the levees were raised. But that meant when the river rose and exceeded the levees, as it did in 1937, the results could be even worse. Major floods happened in 1945, 1973, 1975, 1979, 1983, 1993, 2002, and 2011, which gives the idea that floods are a natural part of the river system.

In fact, floods have always been part of the river. The flow would exceed its channel and deposit sand on its natural levees and rich organic silt in the floodplains. It was a balanced system. But we changed that. Humans created hard surfaces and drainage systems that increased the speed of runoff, and most importantly we created an artificial valley—the levees. Since the time of the glaciers, the runoff to the south spread out over 200 miles, constantly shifting and finding new access to the Gulf. The lower river was a place where distributaries replaced tributaries as the primary channels. Distributaries take water out of the main channel rather than putting it in like tributaries.

When the levees were established, this system of releasing flow was blocked. The river was "controlled" and, of course, the flow went faster, went straighter, and rose within the artificial walls. The problem with these walls is that when the water flowed over, it filled the land and was trapped away from the river by the levee. So the levees keep raising and artificial systems are put in place to relieve the flow. This was good in theory, but weak in relationship to the 200-mile system that once existed. Now many of those bayous and channels lie fallow, not recharged, but still important to waterfowl and natural diversity.

There are still more tributaries within this lower section. The next major river is the Red River, where one of the large diversions is in place to control the flows of both the Mississippi and Red. It also controls the potential diversion of these waters down the Atchafalaya. The Old River Control Structure (Morganza Spillway) allows thirty percent of the waters of the Mississippi to follow the track that should probably be the real channel of the Mississippi River today. In the 1973 flood, the spillway was almost washed out—someday the river may still win the battle.

Or, if not the Atchafalaya, the Mississippi River could jump the Bonnet Carré Spillway and make Lake Pontchartrain its route to the ocean as it did in the past.

Chapter Three

Whether the Weather

MIKE

A<small>NY TRIP IS SUBJECT</small> to the whims of weather, so let's get this fact out of the way right away: call it global warming, climate change, or climate weird-ness—we believe. However, this is not a discussion about the merits of global climate, but rather a look at the weather challenges we faced in a longitudinal travel that would have 2,000 miles of variation. This fact was very apparent on February 25, 2014, as we were writing this chapter. The temperatures at 7:00 A.M. along the Mississippi were as follows:

Lake Itasca: -17° F
St. Cloud: -9° F
Minneapolis: -8° F
Dubuque: 5° F
St. Louis: 27° F
Memphis: 39° F
New Orleans: 61° F

That's a seventy-eight-degree temperature span.

In 2010, we hiked around Lake Superior beginning April 29 after two months of above-average temperatures and a record "no snowflake" March in Minnesota. Then we became concerned in the fall of 2012 when we read in the St. Paul *Pioneer Press*,

ST. LOUIS—From sunken steamboats to a millennium-old map engraved in rock, the drought-drained rivers of the nation's midsection are offering a rare and fleeting glimpse into years gone by. Lack of rain has left many rivers at low levels unseen for decades, creating problems for river commerce and recreation and raising concerns about water supplies and hydropower if the drought persists into next year, as many fear.

In 2013, we planned on canoeing the upper Mississippi in late April and early May, but in April, Minnesota set a snowfall record. We had eighteen inches of snow in Willow River on the eighteenth and eight inches more on the twenty-second. The newspapers reported thirty-six inches of ice on Lake Winnibigoshish and Cass Lake (part of the upper river) on April 29.

In a report on walleye fishing and the May 11 opener in Minnesota, the Minneapolis *Star-Tribune* reported, "Henry Drewes, DNR regional fisheries manager in Bemidji, said twenty-six to thirty-six inches of ice covers Lake of the Woods, Upper Red, Leech and Cass lakes, which are in his region. What are the chances ice will be gone by May 11?"

The Bemidji *Pioneer* reported: "Melting Snow Causes Road Closures. Frozen culverts blocked drainage and the ice on the lakes made a dam for inflowing streams. Ice blocks filled the high water downstream as it made its way towards the Twin Cities."

Since we could not go north, we went south to get on open water between Memphis and New Orleans and watched the river rising with the surge of northern waters from heavy rains in Illinois. The high waters along the Ohio and Illinois rivers converged to raise the Mississippi River to higher levels, challenging the levees.

Jeff Masters, via Weather Underground, wrote on April 19,

It seems like just a few months ago barges were scraping bottom on the Mississippi River, and the Army Corps of Engineers was blowing up rocks on the bottom of the river to allow shipping to continue. Wait, it *was* just a few months ago—less than four months ago! Water levels on the Mississippi River at St. Louis bottomed out at -4.57' on January 1 of 2013, the ninth lowest water level since record keeping began in 1861, and just 1.6' above the all-time low-water record set in 1940 (after the great Dust Bowl drought of the 1930s).

But according to National Weather Service, the exceptional April rains and snows over the upper Mississippi River watershed will drive the river by Tuesday to a height forty-five feet higher than on January 1. The latest forecast calls for the river to hit 39.4' on Tuesday, which would be the eighth greatest flood in history at St. Louis, where

flood records date back to 1861. Damaging major flooding is expected along a 250-mile stretch of the Mississippi from Quincy, Illinois, to Thebes, Illinois, next week."

The weather service made this announcement on Earth Day, April 22: "River gauges are still on the rise in many parts of the Midwest. Much of Northern Illinois, Eastern Iowa, and Northeast Missouri will be hardest hit. In some areas, river levels will approach and even break records." On the same day, *USA Today* wrote:

> Only a few months after a historic dry spell disrupted barge traffic on the Mississippi River, deadly floods brought soggy havoc over the weekend across the upper Midwest, and more flooding is in store this week along many rivers. "Torrential rain last week, concentrated in two days or less, has led to major flooding in parts of the Midwest," said AccuWeather meteorologist Alex Sosnowski. "In some areas, flooding will continue well through the upcoming week."

On April 29, the third anniversary of our Full Circle walk around Lake Superior, the National Weather Service issued this warning for Vicksburg, Mississippi:

The Mississippi River at Vicksburg is currently at 39.0 feet (April 29, 2013, 8:00 A.M. CDT) and rising steadily. The level at Vicksburg is predicted to rise to 40.3 feet on Friday. The current Flood Advisory issued by the National Weather Service in Jackson at 08:22 P.M. CDT Sunday, April 28, 2013, predicts a crest at Vicksburg near 42.0 feet by gauge or 88.23 feet elevation on Saturday, May 11, 2013. This is about one foot below flood stage. Flood stage is 43.0 feet by gauge or 89.23 feet elevation. When river level reaches 40.0 feet, several roads in the Long Lake and Chickasaw Bayou communities are inundated. Elevation (MSL) = 46.23 feet + gauge height.

The *Times-Picayune* in New Orleans reported on April 30:

Rising Mississippi River prompts inspections, restrictions on work near levees. A rising Mississippi River has prompted the Army Corps of Engineers to activate the first phase of its flood-fighting program, including increased levee inspections and restrictions on work within 1,500 feet of any river levee.

On Monday morning, the river had risen to 11.7 feet at the Carrollton Gage in New Orleans. It's expected to crest at fourteen feet on May 16. Water from the river will begin leaking through pins in lower bays of the Bonnet Carré Spillway sometime this week . . .

On May 2, Mike Cole from KHQA (broadcasting to western Illinois, northeastern Missouri, and southeastern Iowa) posted,

> Cold and cloudy across the region currently at 3:00 P.M. Rain will spread across the area tonight. We will see likely rain chances with a COLD rain on tap as temps. fall into the thirties overnight. Cannot rule out some snowflakes mixed in at times out in the far northwestern part of the viewing area, however, the Tri-States in general including Quincy, Hannibal, Macomb, and Keokuk should see just a cold rain that lasts on into the weekend. Locally heavy rains of two to three inches will be expected as we head into Sunday.

In Minneapolis, the locks were closed due to high water. Flood crests along the Illinois and Wisconsin rivers headed downstream.

The Mississippi River is like a series of funnels, which capture lots of water over big areas and concentrates it in to the valley of the Mississippi. This happens with the Minnesota and St. Croix rivers and all the tributaries up north. Then the next big funnel combines the Illinois and Wisconsin rivers with the Iowa River and many smaller tributaries. Finally, the last big funnel is the Missouri and the Ohio, gathering more waters from an even bigger watershed and moving them down to the Mississippi.

The shift of the jet stream (the river of air that flows between the arctic cold air and the tropical hot air masses) to a more southerly flow brought it closer to the gulf. The unfrozen Arctic Ocean did not provide the low temperatures that normally create a more northerly jet stream. The lower latitudinal jet stream flow brought the cold air closer to the Gulf of Mexico's water evaporation. In turn, this increased storm potential as the combined air masses had lower dew points (the level where water molecules form and the air becomes 100% saturated is 100% humidity).

This result was snow up north and massive rain storms in Illinois and Michigan. The ice on the first big lake within the river system, Bemidji, and the largest lake (therefore, the widest place on the Mississippi), Winnibigoshish, both went out on May 17—a record late date. In 2012, Winnie had set a record for the earliest ice out—March 30! The average ice out date is April 27.

Historically, the lower Mississippi had a 200-kilometer floodplain to dissipate the massive volume of water, but now the levees have raised an artificial valley wall to confine the waters for navigation, which means the water levels rise precipitously in response to the gathering waters in

the upstream locations. In one week on the paddlewheel *Queen of the Mississippi*, the river rose over eight feet.

On June 5, 2013, KMOV in St. Louis reported,

> The Mississippi River reached its sixth-highest level in St. Louis on Tuesday as water continues to rise in the area.
>
> "Every Mississippi River gauge in our area is having a top four to six crest on record," said News 4 Chief Meteorologist Steve Templeton. "The river is cresting now for Grafton-Alton-St. Louis.
>
> "The Missouri River has already crested and the Meramec River is causing major flooding in Valley Park and Arnold."
>
> Meanwhile, "the Illinois River is cresting at Harding and is at its third-highest level on record.
>
> "The River Des Peres is already very high due in large part to the back-up caused by the Mississippi River being so high, said Templeton.
>
> "We have seen one levee breach near West Alton, Missouri," Templeton said. "All of this water on our area rivers puts tremendous pressure on our levees."

2013 offered another weather-related crisis—tornadoes. They happen every year when the heat of the Great Plains rises to meet the colder arctic air masses, combining with moisture from the Gulf. They are sudden, devastating, and difficult to predict (prediction potential is better than ever, but the exact time and place is not possible). While a tornado hit just south of Hannibal, Missouri—Mark Twain's boyhood home—on May 21, it was the devastating tornadoes that hit the Oklahoma City area the beginning of June that were historic.

Downstream from New Orleans to the Gulf of Mexico is the Mississippi River Delta (which we have to differentiate from the state of Mississippi delta, the land of cotton and blues fame). The Mississippi (state) delta is between the Yazoo and the Mississippi. The delta of the Mississippi (river) is sometimes referred to as the "bird's foot" because of the unique shape of its final outlet into salt water. This delta was a mass of land interspersed with water but now much of the land mass has disappeared. On the south end of the route, we worry about hurricanes. We have all heard of Katrina—one of the most dramatic hurricanes in the mass media age—and saw the devastation spread across the queen city of the Mississippi as our engineered system met devastating energy from the wind and waves and oceanic surge. These hurricanes are more intense—see Sandy on the East Coast as an example. The hurricanes are intensified by warmer Gulf and ocean water, by sea levels that are rising as the average temperature of the earth increases (water expands as it warms,) and by the lack of vegetation in places like the river delta.

We learned how the dramatic tsunami in the Indian Ocean in 2004 that killed so many and devastated an entire region that included Sri Lanka, Thailand, and Indonesia could have had less impact if the coastal mangroves had not been removed. These simple plants that seem to distract from the beauty of the beach also slow and mitigate the hurricane and tsunami damage. The same is true of New Orleans. Had we not lost land mass the equivalent of Connecticut, the force would have been less, the damage reduced, and the cost far less than what it was.

Traveling in the neighborhoods of New Orleans, we saw the recovery and at the same time the size of the impact, but what we had not realized was that many of the same people who suffered from Katrina in 2005 then suffered from Isaac in 2012. People moved to "safe homes" only to have these second homes destroyed—sometimes because the high water was trapped by the very structures that had been put in place to protect

from another Katrina. The Weather Channel states that "Isaac started as a disturbance coming off western Africa, then took a two-week voyage across the Atlantic Ocean, Caribbean Sea, and Gulf of Mexico."

The mouth of the river has four medusa-like channels that bring the fresh water from what is now the Mississippi River Channel into the Gulf of Mexico. On May 16, 2013, WWNO (New Orleans's public radio station) reported:

> The clang of tide gauges throughout parts of southeast Louisiana aren't from a science fiction movie, though they may make residents feel like they're caught in one.
>
> Those sounds tell the stories of rising tides along the Gulf Coast and melting glaciers in the Arctic. And they tell how scientists believe those two events, taking place thousands of miles apart, are the reasons why the Gulf of Mexico is on pace to submerge most of southeast Louisiana by the end of the century—if nothing is done.
>
> Those are the sounds that explain why climate change is the biggest threat ever to the future of New Orleans and its surrounding landscape.

The devastation that follows these two counterpunches of climate change are caused by steric sea level rise, which in turn is caused by the

increase in volume of heated water and the eustatic sea level change that comes from the ice melts in mountains and polar regions and the resulting increase in volume.

On June 11, 2031, Weather Underground had this headline: "Mississippi River Levels Drop, but Flooding Remains," and Jim Salter wrote,

> ST. LOUIS—The flood-swollen Mississippi River is going down, but it will be some time before things dry out.
>
> The waterway has crested from Iowa through southern Missouri and Illinois, but it remained above flood stage at many spots Monday. Hundreds of thousands of acres of farmland are under water and hundreds of roads remain closed. And water woes could linger in some rural areas for weeks after the flood is technically over.
>
> "It will be a while," National Weather Service meteorologist Mark Fuchs said. "That's particularly true behind areas where levees have broken. A lot of that water's trapped and can't get back into the channel."
>
> Levee breaches from flooding this spring have been limited to mostly small agricultural levees, most of them in rural Missouri north of St. Louis.

Nearly a month later, on July 5, AgFax.com reported, "Over the past several days, heavy rain has resulted in high flows on portions of the Upper Mississippi River. As of July 2, four Mississippi River locks were closed—locks 16, 17, 18, and 20."

On August 6, 2013, *USA Today* ran another story about the situation at the mouth of the river and the range of islands and marshes along the coastal edge of Louisiana:

> *USA Today* traveled to this place where the Mississippi meets the Gulf of Mexico as the sixth stop in a year-long series to explore places where climate change is changing lives.
>
> "The sea is rising and the land is sinking," says Louisiana state climatologist Barry Keim of Louisiana State University in Baton Rouge. "The two together mean that wetlands are disappearing here at unprecedented rates worldwide." Add in the threat of more powerful hurricanes spurred by climate change, Keim says, "and you have to worry about the past repeating itself here."
>
> "Louisiana is, in many ways, one of the best examples of starting to see some of the near-term implications of climate change," says

environmental policy expert Jordan Fischbach, of the Pardee RAND Graduate School in Pittsburgh, part of the team that last year developed tools for the state to decide what coastal restoration projects to pursue. "In some ways, I feel like it is the canary in the coal mine because they are seeing effects that change people's day-to-day lives."

Cemeteries are sinking and washing away in towns like Leeville, Louisiana, on their way to becoming isolated spits of land. Onetime orange groves and cotton fields are now covered with water.

Change here is constant but not subtle, so authorities have embarked on ambitious projects to, actually and figuratively, turn the tide. In May, the Louisiana Coastal Protection and Restoration Authority (CPRA) announced thirty-nine projects it hoped to see reverse the damage, part of a fifty-year, fifty-billion-dollar plan. They range from restoring marshes to spilling fresh river water into the delta to rebuilding barrier islands.

"Every three miles of wetlands restored means one foot less of hurricane storm surge, the water wall pushed ahead of storm winds that is often one of the biggest killers in a hurricane," Keim says.

"I worry a fifty-year plan isn't enough, that it won't be enough," Keim says. "If we were talking about a 500-year plan, or a 1,000-year plan, that might be enough to bring things back."

In August, *Heartland Boating* posted, "Mississippi Marinas Hit Hard."

Probably the hardest hit were the marine businesses on the Mississippi River. By late June, water was above the flood stage in many places for the fourth time. At some locations, people needed secondary boats to get to their primary boats. Gas docks and pump-outs were shut down, and boaters were advised to stay off the water due to strong currents and heavy bacteria.

Cindy Bisek at Red Wing Marina in Red Wing, Minnesota, said that spring "has been a challenge," from snow in May to rain seemingly every other day. There was a lot of debris on Lake Pepin, and a more than two-foot rise in water levels was expected in the week preceding the big Water Ski Days festival in nearby Lake City. The main business at the marina there was pump-outs, as people just sat on their boats at the dock.

At Island City Marina in Sabula, Iowa, owner Jerry Lawson said they only pumped about 200 gallons of gas over the Memorial Day weekend, down from their normal 500 to 600 gallons. Bluff Harbor Marina in Burlington, Iowa, went more than eight weeks without being able to get to some of their slips. Things finally seemed to be settling down as they headed into their major weekend, Steamboat Days, in mid-June, but then they got two and a half inches of rain that Saturday night.

"We haven't had a spring," said Jaime Aslin at Two Rivers Marina in Rockport, Illinois. Late in June, many of their boats were still winterized, as flooding again saturated the area.

Although Port Charles Marina in St. Charles, Missouri, had eighteen inches of water in their office the first time it flooded—then another thirty-one inches later—they stayed busy with yard and mechanical work. Fortunately, they had a nice Fourth of July.

But drought—the flip side of this wavering climate—meant that "in 2011 and 2012, the Kansas Geological Survey reported the average water level in the state's portion of the aquifer dropped 4.25 feet." This was the reason for the low water in fall of 2012 that worried us for nine months before our start downriver. On our travels we saw all the variations, and the amount of sand along the river's edge was amazing. I had never seen so much sand, and it did make for an inviting set of beaches.

However, in the midst of beauty can be hidden dangers. A headline out of St. Louis on August 17 of that year read, "August Drought Exposes Quicksand Along Mississippi River, Missouri River." The Associated Press reported:

A lack of rain in the United States's midsection in recent months has reduced water levels in some of the nation's biggest rivers, exposing sandbars that experts warn could be deadly quicksand.

Steve Barry, emergency management chief for the Corps of Engineers office in Memphis, Tennessee, said the exposed sand looks dry on top but it is really saturated mud. Combined with the undercurrent of water in the fast-moving rivers, that creates a true danger.

"If it's really wet sand and there's flowing water underneath it, that's what quicksand is," Barry said. "The other issue is that as the river flows by, it undercuts. You think you're on a sandbar but you're basically on a ledge. You put enough weight on it and you end up in the river."

. . . an eleven-year-old girl had to be rescued after sand swallowed her up to her waist while she and her family fished along the Mississippi near New Madrid in southeast Missouri. Firefighter Jim Russell said the girl began to sink and the more she struggled, the faster she descended.

On September 4, Paul Huttner on Minnesota Public Radio posted:

"River Weather" Whiplash: Mississippi at St. Cloud shows extreme river level fluctuations in 2013.

It's hard to believe after the spring and early summer deluge, but many rivers are now running near historic lows in central and southern

Minnesota. Check out the latest "hydrograph" from the Mississippi at St. Cloud. At 3.97' it's the fourth lowest level on record . . . and the lowest in twenty-one years, since 1992!

WKYC out of Cleveland, Ohio, offered this October 29, 2013, weather report: "Snow showers developed across the upper Midwest on Tuesday, while rain showers developed just to the south across the mid-Mississippi River valley." In October 2013, I camped in Prairie du Chien, Wisconsin, for a week with the temperature at twenty-three degrees and winds in excess of thirty miles per hour—with snow flurries. I had to stop my excursion in my twelve-foot fishing boat because of safety considerations and physical problems.

Around the same time, the Chicago Weather Center reported, "September went down in the books as the sixth warmest for the contiguous United States, or 2.5° above the twentieth-century average. Temperatures then tumbled in October. October was the thirty-seventh coolest on record, 0.6° below average."

The weather weirdness along the river did not abate in November, either. An outbreak of tornadoes on November 17 was the deadliest in Illinois history, according to a report by Weather Underground, resulting in the deaths of five people in the state, along with three deaths in Kentucky and numerous injuries. The outbreak spawned violent storms in seven states and sent damaging straight-line winds over a larger area, impacting at least five more states.

The Upper Mississippi River Refuge tried to offer an Owl Prowl event and had to cancel both November 15 and 20 because of inclement weather. A month later, on the winter solstice (December 21), the storms were back. Alabama ABC television noted, "The more intense storms are currently crossing the Mississippi River into Mississippi and western Tennessee. The storms are moving to the east rapidly and are producing very gusty winds, torrential rainfall and are bringing with them the threat of damaging winds, tornadoes, and flooding."

In Minnesota, blizzards left close to two feet of snow across the river's source by December 20. We were on the *Queen of the Mississippi* from the Saturday after Christmas through the Saturday after New Year, and the weather continued its craziness with temperatures below freezing in Vicksburg and Natchez and just thirty-six degrees when we came back and stayed in New Orleans.

And if you think that we just chose the wrong year to go, we can only tell you that every year on the Mississippi has its own challenges To prove that, 2014 started out with two "Polar Vortexes." The Weather Channel wrote:

The core of the cold came Monday, January 6, and Tuesday, January 7. Subzero temperatures affected a large swath from Montana to New York and as far south as northern Oklahoma and northern Alabama.

Persistent winds pushed wind chills into life-threatening territory, reaching forty-below to sixty-below zero across a large swath of the Midwest. The National Weather Service in Wilmington, Ohio, said the wind chills were the coldest observed in central and southwest Ohio since 1994 . . . Minneapolis-St. Paul spent sixty-two consecutive hours below zero . . .

Then, to show how things continue to fluctuate, we were supposed to join the paddlewheel in St. Paul in August of 2014 to journey to St. Louis. Because of low water conditions, the paddlewheel could not make it up to St. Paul and we had to take a bus with all the passengers to Dubuque. In an earlier trip in 2014, they could not make it because the water was too high and they could not get under the bridges!

"This is insane. You don't expect peak Mississippi River flooding in early winter," wrote Eric Fischer, CBS Boston's chief meteorologist, to describe 2015. Each year, our travels show us new aspects of this mighty river and remind us that there are more unexpected times to come.

Of the 2015 spring flooding, the Weather Channel wrote,

Record flooding along some tributaries after torrential post-Christmas weekend rain has sent the Mississippi River to levels not seen since the Great Flood of 1993, and that excess water will continue to flow downstream, triggering flooding in the Lower Mississippi Valley into mid-January. Flood crests also continue to roll down several tributaries in the Mississippi River's drainage basin.

The pulse of high water created a record in Cape Girardeau and then down the river. Like a hill within the waterway, this surge of water created problems in city after city. Each watched and waited, prepared, and listened to the reports of their upstream neighbors. Eventually, the Bonnet Carré Spillway had to be opened and water was transported to Lake Pontchartrain, where the salt water fish suffered from a deluge of fresh water.

Chapter Four

Road Trips & College Courses

KATE

Our journey to discover the Mississippi has taken many different forms, with the 477-mile canoe trip/college course that Mike did for Northland College serving as the source of our inspiration. The Northland College journey with a few students started near Palisade in northern Minnesota and went south to La Crosse, Wisconsin. It was intended to begin much further north, but that summer (it was a July trip) the northern sections of the river were dry from drought. We added many other trips with college students and even one with a combination of Russian and American high school students.

The college trip left some lingering memories and river images. There was the campsite in the state forest near Aitkin where a walk down the forest road brought Mike and a couple students to a house with generous owners who invited them in for fresh baked banana bread and ice water.

North of St. Cloud, they played in the Sauk Rapids—the only rapids on the Mississippi River other than the St. Anthony Falls. At St. Anthony Falls was the tallest lock on the river, one that does not have a number. This lock is now closed due to the threat of Asian carp getting to the upper river, but the sense of size was amazing. As the water dropped, the canoes felt like guppies in a fifty-gallon tank.

Below the locks the canoes passed nudists, fishermen, and racing crews through the steep valley. Next, the canoes passed historic Fort Snelling and Pike Island, where Zebulon Pike signed the first Indian treaty in the area. It gave Native American land to the United States government for the building of Fort Snelling. The Minnesota River joins the Mississippi at this junction and the river is wider here and flows unimpeded; therefore, it was open to a history of steamboats and river commerce.

The capitol of Minnesota, St Paul, resides on higher ground and offers a view of the bend in the river that leads to downstream markets, while the city spreads along its banks. We tried to imagine how history would have changed if the community had retained its original name of Pig's Eye—named for Pig's Eye Parrant, who opened a tavern in the caves along the river to serve river men and a few of the soldiers from the fort.

The Full Length Mississippi Journey began on the Great River Road and paralleled places Mike and his students had experienced. We passed places like Red Wing and Wabasha, that were named for Native Americans, and Lake Pepin.

We explored the historic museums of Winona, including the impressive Watkins building. This was nostalgic for Mike since his grandfather had once driven one of their buggies and as a result had acquired the nickname "Doc." The historic house in Homer was where the college students got their best laugh when they saw the bundling board that allowed strangers—men and women—to share a bed. The watermelon they ate on the Winona riverfront on a hot July afternoon matched the banana bread they enjoyed on the upper portion.

In Perrot State Park, three musicians joined Mike's college class at their camp and shared paddlewheel songs by the fire. The only threatening moment on that trip was when a motorboat approached the canoes as they waited at a lock. They were next to the concrete apron that leads to the lock and the boat did not slow down until it came right up to them. They were nearly swamped by the surge of water that sent the canoes crashing against the concrete. They camped below this lock and dam on

an island on the Minnesota shore. In the evening, a barge and tow failed to negotiate the turn and took out a large tree as well as a portion of the shore—a good reminder to camp on the inside of the bend.

In graduate courses that Mike taught in Itasca State Park and along the Whitewater River, he continued to learn more about the Mississippi. A massive display of showy lady slippers in Itasca and Iron Bog Natural and Scientific area will always be an image in his memory, as well as the variety of mussels that we sampled above Wabasha.

With those experiences and a few others in our Mississippi background, we knew we had to make a road trip, one that explored possible bike routes, communities, and river sites and included culture and food.

March 18, 2012

WE LEFT HOME with temperatures in the seventies and high humidity. We had just heard the first eastern bluebird of the year at our house—far earlier than normal—and on the way we saw great blue herons flying over the trees of their rookery. The Snake River still had ice on it, but it was dark in color and obviously close to going out.

Getting closer to St. Paul, we saw a mature bald eagle flying with something in its talons as it landed on a giant stick nest in a large tree. Its mate was perched nearby. People were out on golf courses and in the city many were wearing shorts. Lots of people, we were happy to see, were out riding bikes.

Close to the river, the south wind was so strong that it made the surface appear to flow north with waves curling and white-capped. We crossed over the St. Croix River where it meets the Mississippi in Prescott,

Wisconsin. The main street in town was hopping with big Harley motor-cycles and people milled around outside of pubs and bars, admiring one another's bikes. Just outside of town is the Mississippi River Visitor Center, where families with little kids used the playground while adults walked down to the overlook and gazed at the big, dark, corrugated river. Each river town we drove through had a cluster of bikers in front of a "watering hole" and when they all roared out of town as a herd, they sounded like a colossal jet taking off. In Stockholm (my favorite small town on the Wisconsin side) I put my hands over my ears as I stood on the corner, with the sounds from their pipes reverberating through my body.

In Stockholm, Mike discovered a pie shop on the corner and couldn't resist. He ordered a slice of fruit pie while I swooned over the gorgeous Indian-style blouses at the gallery across the street. We can always be counted on to support the local economies. We both went away happy and satisfied. The temperature had reached seventy-nine degrees!

There were lots of hills on the Wisconsin side of the river and we measured their lengths, thinking about what it would be like to ride up or fly down them on bikes. Then I looked at the fairly narrow shoulder on either side of the road and imagined what it would be like with big semis blowing past.

On our left, the big limestone and sandstone cliffs rose into the sky, drawing our eyes upward, just as the kettles of turkey vultures were drawn to them by the rising thermals. Lake Pepin was on our right, dark and choppy, with a humid haze hovering over the narrows between the bluffs on the far end.

Mike was reminded of countless canoe trips he has taken on the river and I thought about the houseboat trips I'd been on. We both have a long history with this river.

By the time we reached Nelson, Wisconsin, we saw green grass and willow trees beginning to leaf out. It reached a high of eighty-one degrees and was still that temperature at 6:00 P.M. when we reached Doug White's house in Onalaska. We hadn't seen Doug or his wife, Theresa, and their son, Harrison, for ten years. Last time, they were living in Dallas and Theresa was about at the end of the pregnancy that produced their daughter, Alexa, who greeted us at the door. Doug had invited Jan Wellik, one of Mike's former Hamline graduate students, to come to dinner. She arrived with her husband, Mike, and baby boy, Trey.

After dinner we visited with Doug and Theresa in the sunroom and Mike detailed all of his ailments for Doug since he is a physician (rheumatologist and researcher) and had agreed to be our medical advisor on the bike trip. We also had a big discussion about Lyme disease with him. Doug's colleague at the hospital was doing research on ticks and Lyme, and feels the main reason the ticks (and disease) are spreading is climate change and the lack of extended subzero temps, which we can believe. He also talked about the fact that the bacteria (*borellia sp.*) is mutating. He believes in the future we will see really weird symptoms in people who have late stages of the disease.

March 19

WE LEFT ONALASKA, Wisconsin, around 9:00 A.M. with the temperature at sixty-six degrees and cloudy skies. Rain looked imminent, but we didn't see any until around noon in Prairie du Chien, and it cleared up as we drove down the Iowa side of the river.

We crossed the bridge from Wisconsin into Minnesota near La Crescent and stopped at a Minnesota rest area managed cooperatively with United States Fish and Wildlife Service (USFWS) and Army Corps of Engineers. A big kettle of turkey vultures was slowly circling near the top of a bluff and we saw some hawks flying in duets. The surrounding trees were full of cardinals, robins, red-winged blackbirds, grackles, and even a song sparrow in full-throated song. It is always a beautiful sound when we first hear it in the springtime.

I told Mike I wanted to go to Lansing, Iowa, to a store called Horsfall's. It is an amazing, jam-packed (over one million items, according to their ads) variety store in a ramshackle, run-down-looking wooden building on the main street. Out in front were some sagging, wooden plank "tables"

covered with cardboard boxes of plastic flowers and other knick-knacky stuff. Once inside the store I barely got past the front door because this is where they have put all the scrapbooking supplies. Paper, clear stamps, stickers, and other fun and useful products filled boxes. The deals were so great, it was hard to stop. Mike took photos up and down the main street, which is a true river town lined with red-brick buildings. Like many of these river towns, it has a wonderful old-timey feel and look to it.

Most river towns began with wooden construction, but fires were the bane of early towns and those that started in one structure would quickly become major conflagrations. The wood supply along the river became more valuable for the steam engines that needed a constant supply of fuel for their boilers, and then became just as valuable for the railroad engines. Mud was available for building and it was free. Other than the straw that was used to bind it, it was also fireproof. The additional benefit was that it did not deteriorate in water. Today we see the brick towns along the river and enjoy a sense of history.

At Marquette, Iowa, we crossed back over the river into Wisconsin to meet with Jon "Hawk" Straver at Simply Coffee in Prairie du Chien. John Straver is a big guy with a thick head of gray hair, glasses, and goatee and mustache, and he was more than happy to share his experiences with wildlife along the river. Most recently he had worked with the National Audubon Society. He told us,

> I have been researching birds in this region for thirty-two years. I specialize in red-shouldered hawks, which is a floodplain bird that needs clean water. It lives in the swampy backwaters and needs old growth along the Mississippi River. It's pretty common in this region, but if you get outside this region it is pretty rare. And then recently, [I've specialized in] Cerulean warblers, neo-tropical migrants that come a long distance to get here and nest in large trunks. We have a really dynamic population here.
>
> I have always been interested in clean water and with people who are engaged with clean water and the environment. I have been working in this area since the late seventies in the spring and fall, but fifteen years ago I moved up here.
>
> Some red-shoulders over-winter here, but most return in mid-February. I think my birds are photo-period birds and not temperature. They lay their eggs the last of March or first few days of April. Some are banded, but most aren't. I do my work by territory.

I asked about their life expectancy and John responded, "Seventy percent do not make it one year, but if they make it through that first year, most

are good for six to eight to ten years. I have one nest with the same female that has been good for thirteen years, but I think that is sort of the exception."

The Cerulean warblers wouldn't be back until around the tenth of May, too late to see them on this trip.

We left Prairie du Chien and crossed back to the Minnesota side, continuing to follow the Mississippi River Trail (MRT) route recommended in the bicycling guidebook. It took us to McGregor, Iowa, one of the prettiest of the river towns on this stretch. Built on a slope leading up the bluff, the main street is lined with the brick-and-board storefronts, which include lodging, restaurants, and an assortment of shops, all fronted by elevated sidewalks.

The guidebook suggested going up onto the top of the bluff outside of town that goes by Pike's Peak State Park. Mike camped with one of his college classes in the park, and he loved the forest and the elevation above the river. This road goes almost all the way to Dubuque. It was highly (literally) scenic, since the land drops away to the broad river valley. We drove through several small towns, including Balltown and Sherrill. This part of Iowa is loaded with long glacial hills.

March 20

OUR MISSISSIPPI RIVER TRAIL guidebook really helped us get through Dubuque and onto the road to St. Donatus, where I wanted lunch at the Kalmes Restaurant and Store, featured in the book *Feasting on Asphalt* by TV food personality Alton Brown. The town was settled by people from Luxembourg in the 1850s and one family built a bar and restaurant; the fifth generation of Kalmes continues the tradition. Some of their specialties are from Luxembourg, others are Iowa traditions, and some are a blend of both. Mike had the pork tenderloin sandwich and liked it a lot. I ordered broasted chicken livers with buttered noodles on the side. I have a broad palate and like to try lots of odd recipes. The noodles were like spaetzle, but tossed with butter and crushed saltine crackers. The livers were too deeply fried for my taste and the noodles were okay, but too butter-greasy. It satisfied my curiosity, at least.

We were driving into strong and gusty southerly winds again. The river near the town of Bellevue looked brown and muddy, such a contrast to the Lake Superior water we walked around in 2010. In Clinton, Iowa, at the north end of town, big earthen levees prevented us from seeing the river, but there is a bike trail on top. The other end of town is a major industrial area with an ADM plant—all steel and aluminum pipes and stacks—and a huge golden sphere containing God knows what. It was probably our imagination, but my throat felt scratchy and made me wonder what chemicals were emanating from those towers and smokestacks.

The next town, Princeton, is built right along the river's edge. Here the grass was already a bright green. Out on the water the waves rose up wearing white caps.

Le Clair was a lovely river town. It seemed positively upscale compared to others we'd passed through. Cherry trees had been planted along the boulevard, each encircled by a fancy, wrought-iron fence. The eighty-one-degree temperatures and strong sun made our northern blood simmer when we got out of the car.

Mike found the small, purple-flowered creeping Charlie in bloom when he took a picture of a tug pushing barges upstream north of Buffalo, Iowa. We could not get over how green everything looked. The redbud trees were outstanding and ethereal in appearance.

March 21

IT WAS SIXTY-FIVE DEGREES and overcast when we left the hotel in the morning. And glory be! No wind! We headed across the river hoping to avoid the big storms to the south of us, which was causing flooding in Louisiana and Arkansas. The redbud trees continued to astound us. Their color is almost neon pink or purple or fuchsia and the flowers appear to grow directly out of the branches, outlining them in the process. It reminds me of the creosote shrubs in the desert, only their flowers are yellow.

As we crossed over the river we could see a big hydropower plant near the lock just upriver from the bridge and wondered why there aren't more hydro plants along this big river, instead of all the coal-fired ones.

Some daffodils had already finished blooming. As we drove along this two-lane blacktop road into Warsaw, the limestone cliffs on our left were covered with forest that was showing more and more green, interspersed with wild forsythia shrubs glowing yellow in the grayish light. The town of Warsaw looked pretty bleak, with many empty storefronts.

The bicycle route took us through flat agricultural lands—the old, vast river bottoms. Far in the distance we could see the dark hills of the

Missouri shore. It is always mind-boggling to look across from one set of
hills on the west to those on the east and realize that at one time, when
the glaciers were melting up north, this space was filled with water.

We couldn't see much of the river until we got to Quincy, Illinois. In
one quiet slough was a flock of pelicans, and further on we spotted a big
flock of snow geese (both the white and blue phases) in a farm field.

Quincy is a nice river town built on a hill named for former president
John Quincy Adams and is located in Adams County. The brick buildings
stand tall above the river. Woodland Cemetery is a strange highlight, but
this is one worth visiting with its many historic graves, soldiers' monument, and some very old trees. It sits on top of a bluff with a magnificent
view of the Mississippi River. The land has the same uneven texture that
would have been found throughout the city before it was graded.

This is a memorable town for me because some years ago, when we
were working on our book *Grandparents Illinois Style*, we came through
and stopped at a bike shop for some small items, and I left with a beautiful, "stylin'" new Trek hybrid bike, a nice cross between mountain bike
and street bike, a sweet pale yellow with leather handgrips and seat and
flower designs on the frame. I fell in love immediately and still find it the
most comfortable bike I have ever owned.

Driving out of town on a narrow two-lane road we passed agricultural industrial plants to the right. We wanted to mail a couple postcards, and our guide book told about an unusual post office in Kinderhook, Illinois. Sure enough, it was the most unique little post office building we've ever seen—built entirely of rocks, marbles, stoneware bottles and other miscellanea.

It had been the garage of a Dr. Dechow, who lived in the house next door (which is no longer there). In the late 1920s and early '30s when times were hard, people paid the doctor, who was a rockhound, with pretty or unique rocks. He also built a short wall along the sidewalk that looks like a reef on the prairie. Unfortunately, as so often happens, uncaring thieves have pried some of the special pieces out of the concrete. This is one post office we *really* hope isn't closed, though it's on the list. Only 200-some people live in town, but what a loss it would be.

I spent a lot of time looking closely at the rocks—many were geodes or quartz—and Mike took photos and a video. Inside, the postmistress, Mick Weir, told me this story:

> The building was built originally by Dr. Dechow. He was an old country doctor, and actually he brought me in to the world, so I feel very honored to be here in this building, and I've been here for eighteen

years. He was a rockhound and he loved all kinds of different rocks from all over the world.

Many people paid for his services, such as childbirth, by giving Dr. Dechow rocks to put in the building when he was building it. The rock wall in front of the building was built by him, also, and they said by the time he finished every child in Kinderhook contributed some kind of an artifact or memento.

The post office moved in here in the 1950s, I believe. Now the post office is up for closing. In 1993, it was chosen as one of the most unique post offices in the United States.

South of Kinderhook, the shrubbery was noticeably greener, with more leaves visible on the trees. We drove along rolling hills with little to no traffic, which was a good thing because there was no shoulder on the road. Dandelions bloomed along the edge and we saw our first mockingbird of the trip.

A ferry carried us across the Illinois River at Brussels. The man who motioned us forward said, "I didn't even hear you"—referring to our electric engine, which led to more discussion about Prius cars and then, of course, the weather. He commented about how the last five years or so had been very strange.

In Illinois, we merged onto a road near Pere Marquette State Park, one of our favorite places. We were here in the early spring and remembered our impressions of the stunning, flowering trees. A good bike trail starts in the park and goes to the town of Alton. At 1:00 P.M. the temperature had reached seventy-seven degrees, and there was still a hazy overcast sky with a strong south wind. We watched a tug pushing twelve barges into big, white-capped waves.

The big arch in St. Louis, Missouri, came into view as we tried to find our way through East St. Louis. After some wrong guesses and turns, and requesting help from another motorist waiting at a light next to us, we finally found our way out to Cahokia and then after another wrong turn managed to accidently find ourselves on the right road. Cahokia is a world heritage site, which held a Native American population

believed to have been over 25,000—and some guess a lot more—in 1250 CE, making it larger than most European cities at the time. This large site was developed by a very advanced culture and represents an image of early America that is much different than most history books portray.

An impressive museum portrays life as historians have been able to reconstruct from artifacts. Outside are large mounds—not the pyramids of the Mayans but rather earth platforms raised over 100 feet high to support houses and other structures. Agricultural and sports fields were nearby, lower than the mounds.

At 3:00 P.M. it was seventy-nine degrees, and we saw our first flowering dogwoods—another phenological note for us. One of the things we have done for years is keep track of the first flowers and first birds of each species. This practice is called phenology and is both fulfilling and illuminating. Through our years of records, we have been able to track the overall climactic shifts.

On the river we saw barges loaded to the brim with coal, and earlier we'd seen a bulldozer driving on top of a mountain of coal, the dust curling up behind and blowing away. We wondered about the people living nearby.

As we neared Cairo, we saw farmers spreading fertilizer on their fields. Golden-yellow mustard spread like a blanket beneath an orchard of pecan trees. As if it were a mustard flower fluttering by, a yellow sulfur butterfly tilted back and forth past our car.

March 22

IT WAS GRAY and rainy and the temperature was a cool, pleasing fifty-four degrees. We took some two-lane roads down to New Madrid (*Mād*-rid) past fields with standing water. We couldn't tell if they were rice, cotton, or sorghum fields.

Mike has always wanted to come here because of its historic geologic importance. This is where the mid-continent earthquakes occurred in 1811–1812, including a massive quake that reshaped the Mississippi River and created Reelfoot Lake in one of its fissure zones.

No measurements could be made of the earthquakes, but geologists believe they were the strongest that have ever hit the United States. Estimates put the three primary quakes at eight on the Richter scale and many of the hundreds of aftershocks in the six and seven range. Legend has the Mississippi River running upstream for three days—something that probably did not happen, but the movement of the river, the crevasses on the land, and the stranded old channels need no exaggeration.

We had to find Dorena in order to take a ferry across the Mississippi, but we couldn't figure out a good route without backtracking. At a gas

station, Mike started chatting with a guy who sounded like Bill Clinton. Finally, Mike asked if he knew how to get to Dorena. He assured us he did and could give us better directions than others. First he recited them (and I took notes), then Mike asked him to write them down, which he did; a very helpful chap. But as we found with many people we met on our walk around the lake, people want to be helpful, but they don't always know the current conditions or possible changes that have occurred.

We were told to drive into town and out to the levee, where there was a tourist viewing platform. Then we were to drive up onto the levee (drove our Prius to the levee and the levee was wet—it was raining) and it would be gravel (it was). From there, we'd take a right and go about four miles until we got to a spillway (which we never found), take another right onto a paved road to another levee, and then left into Dorena. Unfortunately, the first paved road on the right was closed to all except local traffic. So we just kept driving on the levee looking at our GPS, which showed the road continuing. We kept following it as it curved around more fields and came to other county roads which we took, blindly aiming for where we thought Dorena should be. This included County Road 00, which ended at the edge of some farm fields. Good thing we didn't have a timeline to meet.

Along the way we saw our first purple wisteria draped lushly over a lamp pole in front of a yard. These remind me of a cross between sweet pea flowers and lilacs—truly a southern flower in my mind. Mike caught sight of a barred owl with a freshly caught mouse in its talons. An eastern meadowlark flew off a power line near us and coasted down near a little pond where one soggy-looking immature bald eagle perched on a snag.

At this same spot, four lesser yellowlegs (our first shorebirds) flapped across the road and landed in the wet field to our left. This should have been a good trip for shorebirds, based on the time of year and habitat we'd be in. The question was whether the odd weather had already pushed them further north.

We spent at least an extra hour wandering about until we finally found Dorena and our route to the ferry landing. It looked abandoned, and we scanned the river in front of us, hoping to see some sign of activity. A sign on a post told us the times of day the ferry operated, and there had been signs along the way saying it was open, but it sure looked deserted now. On the back side of the post was a big red button to push to call for service.

Mike pushed it and then looked up to see another sign that said, "The call button is not working, please call . . ."—a number that had been partially washed away in the rain.

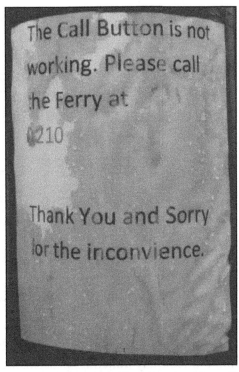

We had seen a tug-type boat and what looked like a ferry across and further up the river, but it disappeared behind an island. Mike tried calling another number listed on the metallic sign, but got a recording about the times of service. Trying again, he finally reached a live human who said they would send a ferry for us, and it would take about twenty minutes. It wasn't too bad being stuck there in a car, knowing we could drive away if need be, but if you had ridden all these backroads on a bike to reach the ferry and found it inoperable, it would be a very discouraging and long ride backtracking.

The same tug and ferry that had gone behind the island now began to cross the river toward us. It had started to rain lightly, so I took refuge in the car while Mike took some video footage of it arriving. Now there is a fee for the service. We couldn't imagine how it could pay for itself, since we were the only car going to the Kentucky side and it cost us fourteen dollars. Pedestrians pay one dollar (who would ever walk across here?) and bikes cost two dollars.

We stood on the deck of the ferry in the wind and mist and looked down at the chocolate milk–colored water and the logs bobbing up and down in front of and to the sides of the ferry. Once we got off and back onto the road, we found ourselves in a very rural area. The first home we passed had the good ol' Confederate flag flying at half-mast. Welcome to the South.

Low-lying fields on either side were covered in either dark-green vegetation or standing water. We encountered a small box turtle resting in the middle of our lane. "Stop," I said. I will never pass by a turtle in the

road if it is possible to move them. Since this was a very quiet road, we backed up, and I hopped out to move the little reptile. It saw me coming and immediately pulled its head inside its high domed shell, hissing for good measure. Then it closed the bottom plastron and sealed itself away from danger. Mike had hoped to get a photograph of its head, but had to settle for the brown and yellow marked shell of the box turtle.

I carried it over to the side of the road it had been pointed at and hoped it would continue on into the safe-looking shrubbery. On the other side of the road, a small white dog on a line ran back and forth yapping

loudly at the damn Yankees.

Overhead, our first black vulture cruised by. Not long after we came to Reelfoot Lake, with its forest of semi-aquatic cypress trees. It was a moody scene of gray mist and rain over dark water and silent bass boats drifting across the surface. We love cypress trees. They are so different from what we are used to, with their deeply flanged trunks that disappear into the dark water and their moss-draped upper branches. Near the lake, purple irises bloomed in people's gardens.

It was lunch time by now and in Tiptonville, Tennessee, Mike pulled into a gas station and went in to find some grub. He came back out with a white bag and pulled out a foil-wrapped sandwich. On it was written "fried bologna and cheese." This is sort of an inside joke related to our walk around Lake Superior, where in Michigan I was inspired by a rural restaurant menu that offered bologna sandwich on white bread—a childhood staple. For the rest of the trip I often had just that for lunch. When I saw this version I remembered my mom actually frying thick bologna pieces, too—or maybe that was SPAM. At any rate, this meat-and-cheese sandwich on pure white, soft bread satisfied my hunger (as much as it may turn your stomach).

After passing Ridgely, the route took us past more levees and low fields. At Porter Gap, we dropped down into a low spot that had hills completely covered in brown (last year's) kudzu, another icon of the south (for northerners). But the flowering trees continued to wow us with their shades of pastel pink flowers.

The sky had begun to clear a bit and was completely sunny by 1:45. It was seventy-two degrees when we left Tennessee behind and entered Mississippi. Then it was onto I-55 and high-speed freeway driving. The last time we were on this route, in 1991, I was astounded by the amount of forest (seemingly spared of development) along the freeway. There was a mix of coniferous and deciduous trees. This was not how I had imagined Mississippi would look. We have always prided ourselves on our great north woods, but nearly the entire way down the state to Jackson we had these big, beautiful forests beside us. Maybe just beyond there are cleared fields, but the trees form a solid green corridor along this highway. Even better, billboards are almost nonexistent.

Once in Jackson, we started seeing bright pink, fully flowered azalea shrubs. We have the northern version at our house and I dream of having them bloom as profusely as these southern beauties.

March 23
Jackson, Mississippi to New Orleans, Louisiana

WE WERE ONLY two and half hours from New Orleans, so we decided to give ourselves a slow morning.

Mike said he heard a fish crow calling when we came out to our car, and we spotted our first palm tree on a boulevard. Mike wanted to take photos of the state capitol, an impressive stone edifice encircled by great live oak trees and other southern species.

Chimneyville looked to be a soul-food focused place. I chose the battered and fried catfish, turnip greens, black-eyed peas, and cornbread. Mike ordered the beef brisket, black-eyed peas, and squash casserole. We also ordered a side of coleslaw. Neither of us had ever had the peas—they were good, although we thought they needed some hot sauce. The greens had a strange aftertaste; the squash casserole was good, as well the catfish. The sweet iced tea was too sweet, and I had to add regular tea.

This place was popular with both white and black folks. Since arriving in the Deep South, we had not noticed any difference in the interactions or relationships between the races. It may be superficial, but everyone seems to be going about their lives cooperatively and respectfully. Those of us in the north may still imagine the south as a place of separation, but based on what we were seeing, it isn't.

We left Jackson full and happy. We knew the afternoon was going to be a straight shot to New Orleans, and once again the sides of the highway were heavily forested until we got just north of the Big Easy and started to see water mixed with fields and forests. Then we were on an elevated highway for miles and miles, looking out at water that we couldn't quite place on our map (Lake Pontchartrain). Here we saw our first great egret slowly flapping over the water. Then the skyscrapers of the city below sea level began to appear. Our GPS did a pretty good job of leading us to the Holiday Inn, just near  the Superdome, which we would describe as a giant tire and wheel.

Our destination on this road trip was National Audubon Society training for volunteers from the Mississippi Flyway. It began with a dinner and presentation by the regional vice president, Chris Canfield. He spoke with passion and optimism for the causes Audubon represents, as well as a return to an emphasis on birds and their habitat. We would also learn a great deal about the Restore Act, which had recently passed the Senate—a huge victory that promises to do much to restore that which was destroyed or badly injured by the BP oil spill. This part of our country has been slowly degrading as the river has been forcibly channeled. First Katrina and then the oil spill really stressed the entire system. It is a long way from Minnesota, but we are closely connected ecologically through our songbirds and waterfowl, especially our state bird, the loon.

March 24 and 25
New Orleans

THE TWO DAYS in New Orleans were filled with training sessions. The National Audubon Society with its new president, David Yarnold, has reconfigured the organization under the flyways of the United States. The Mississippi River is one of the four flyways, and its importance to migratory birds cannot be overstated.

We humans have really messed things up in terms of the ecology and health of this massive riverine system. And it began as soon as Europeans started to settle the region in the late 1600s. Once major cities were built, the river had to be forcibly chained to the route we wanted. Controlling this river is a never-ending task and one at which we will ultimately fail, unless we make some significant changes to the current system of control.

One of the obvious challenges is getting people all along the flyway to care about this situation. The further you live from the Gulf of Mexico, the less you understand—and, dare I say, care—about its future. But if you like to hunt waterfowl, or if you like to see loons on your lake, or if you like the bluebirds who come back to your yard every year, you have to care about the Gulf region, where all of these birds (and hundreds more) stop during migration or spend the winter months. And there are important economic reasons to care for those who aren't into birds. The Gulf is where roughly forty percent of all the commercial seafood in the lower forty-eight states is produced. And more than twenty-five percent of the nation's waterborne exports pass through Louisiana ports alone.

Saturday ended with dinner at Arnaud's in the French Quarter. It is a fabulous old (1918) restaurant made up of thirteen homes that have been cobbled together over the years to make an establishment that today could seat 1,000 people at one time. The original owner's daughter sold the place in 1978, and since then it has been upgraded and improved to become one of the most famous eateries in the Quarter. Our main server was a man from Australia who not only brought our food to us, but also gave a historic recounting of the hotel and the characters who once frequented it. Photographs of celebrities with the proprietors lined the walls in the hallways. The restaurant is as much a museum as a place to eat.

The original restaurant was started by "Count" Arnaud before he moved to the current site, where it combines with Galatoire's and Antoine's to give Bourbon Street its gourmet anchors. Arnaud had been born in the French village of Bosdarros on the outskirts of Pau with no official title attached to his person. He came to the United States and found that he lacked the English to enter medical school so instead went to Stanislaus College in Bay St. Louis on the Gulf of Mexico, in the state of Mississippi. New Orleans, just thirty minutes away, reminded him of his hometown and caused him to want to settle there. He ended up leasing the Old Absinthe House beginning in 1902 and serving French food with a little bottle of wine. In New Orleans when you get something extra it is called "*lagniappe*," and that was his wine. From there he went on to Arnaud's and set a standard that is still a must-eat, must-see location.

After dinner we decided to walk around a bit and found ourselves on Bourbon Street, the wildest street in the entire country, I think. After a few blocks an idea flashed in my mind, and I told Mike, "This place is like the Midway of the State Fair from Hell." Music blasted out of open doorways, where nearly naked women performed undulating invitations to the google-eyed men who stumbled past. Garishly costumed street performers drew crowds and camera flashes. Tourists carried slopping plastic cups of beer, or other concoctions, and teenage girls squealed as rows

of young men tossed strings of colored beads down on them from the balconies. We're not in Kansas anymore, honey (or Minnesota, for that matter). Talk about the Devil's playground! We wove our way through the clusters of gawkers, hucksters, and hawkers for a few blocks, and then I suggested, "Let's get off this and onto some of the side streets."

Mike had wanted to see Preservation Hall, the famous jazz emporium. We found it, but it was closed for a private event. On the other streets of the Quarter are interesting shops selling art, clothing, and other intriguing merchandise, and I enjoyed window shopping. When we got away from the maelstrom of Bourbon Street, we could also see and appreciate the very old architecture. This is the area that was first settled, because it is on the highest land—a bump, really, but high enough to keep it dry during Hurricane Katrina. There's no question there is a romance to this town, and it's easy to see why artists and performers are drawn here. But we also know that in the heat and humidity of summer it would be unbearably oppressive, at least for a couple of northerners like us.

Sunday morning, after a final gathering of attendees and closing comments by the Audubon staff, we boarded a tour bus for a field trip out to Barataria Bayou/Jean Lafitte National Historical Park and Preserve, located a few miles southwest of downtown New Orleans. One thing you can count on when you go to a national park or preserve is recycling bins. We are all too familiar with the difficulty of finding places that recycle once we leave Minnesota. I asked one of the Audubon staffers, David Ringer, who lives in Baton Rouge, about Louisiana's system, and he said they do have curbside, so we asked if we could give him our recycling. It's crazy, but I just can't in good conscience throw things away that I know can be recycled.

At Jean Lafitte, we were met by a former employee of the park who would be our guide on the walk. He explained the geology and ecology of the preserve in a clear and comprehensive way as we stopped at different viewpoints. We were delighted to hear and see Parula warblers and a Prothonotary warbler. Both come to Minnesota, but are difficult to see. Our guide was able to call these species in very close and Mike got some fantastic photographs. They are gorgeous birds—the Parula is a mix of blue, yellow, and rust, while the Prothonotary has a deep, glowing yellow body with black wings and beady black eyes. Everyone was getting a sore neck craning backward to look at the birds overhead.

But our eyes were also drawn to the ground next to the paved trail and boardwalk, where banded watersnakes rested or slipped through the dark water. Several young (and small) alligators floated and basked among the thick vegetation. One of our group members spotted squirrel tree frogs we'd been hearing, clinging to the backsides of leaves next to the boardwalk. These little frogs are bright chartreuse green, and perfectly matched the leaves they clung to.

Red-shouldered hawks, Carolina chickadees, and wrens, tufted titmouse, red-winged blackbirds, and cardinals completed our bird list. It wasn't the abundance we'd hoped for, but it included some very special ones. The migration of the tropical songbirds had not happened yet because they are tied into the photoperiod, and we were still a bit too early for that.

We were pleased to see lots of people, including families with kids and from all ethnic backgrounds, out on the trails. While we seemed to be the only ones using binoculars, we were still glad to know that people were taking advantage of this rich preserve and getting their bodies moving.

As the sun began to set we drove to the water's edge to look for some new birds. Mainly we saw the black-headed laughing gulls—lots of them—sitting on the wooden docks that poked out from the sea wall. On the other side of the road were signs of the hurricane's devastation: lots with just cement pads and grass growing up in the cracks, skeletal remains of trees, a plastic slide for a pool that no longer held water. But there were also new homes that had obviously been built since Katrina.

Beautiful homes of one or two stories rested on concrete or brick stilts at least one or two stories high. These people had decided to tempt fate.

As we looked across the water we could see oil refineries with smoke or flames issuing from their stacks day and night. Not the kind of scenery we'd want to spend hundreds of thousands of dollars to see from a fancy new house. We also spotted a pair of eared grebes floating on the quick-silver-colored water. These are waterfowl that migrate north in the spring.

The sun went down, coloring the sky a deep pink edged with orange and Mike captured it with a couple of gulls silhouetted in flight. Perfect.

Chapter Five

Returning North

KATE

March 26
Bay St. Louis and Pascagoula Audubon Center

Wᴇ ɢʀᴀʙʙᴇᴅ ᴀ ᴄᴏᴜᴘʟᴇ of (way too expensive) sandwiches and drove down the shoreline looking for a nice beach where we could eat al fresco. What we found was major construction. They were building sea walls all along this part of Bay St. Louis. We only found one public beach still available, so we pulled into the parking lot. Laughing gulls were in an uproar over some food that had been spilled or dumped on the asphalt. A roofed structure with some park benches beneath it was where we sat and ate. Mike wandered with his camera, but we couldn't see any shorebirds at this location, so we got back in the car and started heading east on I-90.

This is where we encountered moving sand dunes. The beach was to our right, but it was spreading into the right lane of the two-lane road we were driving on. Intersections between the eastbound and westbound lanes also had large deposits of sand. We'd never seen anything like it on this shore—and both of us have been here a couple times. We wondered what was causing it and at one point I said, "Looks like they need a snow-plow." Just a few minutes later we saw dump trucks lined up one behind the other, with a plow and another vehicle that seemed to suck up the piles made by the plow, deposit them onto a conveyor belt, and from there into the bed of one of the dump trucks. Later, we learned that this situation occurred because of the storms a couple weeks earlier, and that it happens regularly during spring storms. In fact, the white sand that runs parallel with the road for miles is not natural. It has been dredged up from the gulf and placed there to make the beach. Our guess is that this shoreline was once all mangrove swamp—the best form of protection from hurricanes and also the best nursery for fish.

Looking to our right and scanning for shorebirds, we saw instead brown pelicans, the first of our trip. Some flew low over the water, just barely skimming it, while others swooped upward and then plunged bill first into the water, in search of a fish or two. Finally, we decided to park the car and walk for a bit on the white sand. Down at the surfline, the water swished in and out, a muddy-silty soup, with a lot of organic matter and odd bits of plastic floating in it. All we could see was the stark contrast between the crystal-clear waters of Lake Superior and this Gulf of Mexico. One can't help but wonder about the health of all the creatures whose only home is in these waters.

I read an article about the crabbers—those who catch blue crabs—and how the harvest is one of the worst ever this year. For many of these multi-generational fishermen, this could be the year that seals their fate and ends their livelihoods. Not that they will get much attention in other parts of the country, but it signals a loss not only to a deep part of the culture of the coast, but an indication that something is terribly wrong in the ecosystem. Blue crabs not only feed us, but a host of other animals in the food chain.

At the Pascagoula River Audubon Center we met Director Mark LaSalle. He had arranged for us to speak that evening at the local community college about our walk around Lake Superior, as part of their annual speaker's series

leading up to the Pascagoula River Festival. Mark is an ebullient man with a quick, broad smile. He immediately reminded me of Stephen Colbert in appearance, but with a much thicker southern accent. He is also a passionate lover of nature.

The center consisted of a small, older house and the surrounding wetland forest. A cluster of bird feeders stood outside the windows of the house, with lots of cardinals flying in and out. Nearby was a tall wooden structure, with a smaller, square top, like a chimney. In fact, that is exactly what it is designed to replicate. This is a demonstration project to attract chimney swifts, small swallow-like birds that historically roosted and nested in tall hollow trees. With the loss of old trees, the birds switched to chimneys of all sizes. Over time,

people have become annoyed or concerned about fire hazards and have blocked the birds' access to their chimneys, leaving the birds with fewer and fewer options, ultimately leading to fewer and fewer chimney swifts. Like the very successful efforts to bring back the eastern bluebird with special houses for them, Mark hopes the same might happen for the swifts.

March 27
Bay St. Louis to Metaire

WITH THE WEATHER SUNNY and seventy-five degrees, we headed back to the Pascagoula (a Choctaw word meaning "bread-making") River for a boat tour of the bayous and river itself. Mark LaSalle had arranged for us to take this tour and we welcomed the chance to get on the water and see this landscape with a fresh perspective. The boat, a flat-bottomed aluminum craft with an

awning and benches that faced out on either side, was completely full with other adults and some homeschooled kids and their parents. Captain "Beanie" McCoy, a middle-aged man with a lifetime of experiences on the river and its backwaters, would be our guide. For two hours he shared his knowledge and enthusiasm of this land and waterscape with us. We were at the back of the boat and the only passengers with binoculars.

The Pascagoula is a tidal river with brackish water. It is popular with fishermen because they can catch both freshwater and saltwater fish, like catfish or flounder. He told us about one fisherman who had a tug of war with an alligator over a catfish on his line. Unsure whether he was pulling our leg or not, the captian said it happens. Then he showed us a bar of soap they use to catch the fish. He said some people use Dial, but he had a bar made in Mexico that works much better. They cut it into lots of pieces and put it on the line. We were dumbfounded, but he said, "If you look  at the label, you'll see that it's about sixty percent fats." He also told us they catch mullet, known locally as Biloxi bacon; it was served for breakfasts during the Depression years as "fish and grits."

On either side of the boat we passed acres of sawgrass, juncus (rush), and blue flag irises. One of the most surprising pieces of information we learned was about the wild rice that grows in this river. What? We thought northern Minnesotans were the only ones who could claim that plant. But no, there was wild rice down here, close to the Gulf. We were told they are rarely able to harvest any though, because the redwing blackbirds get it all before the humans can.

Beanie started commenting on the amount of water in the river. The tide was coming in, but it is never very big; most of the water causing the rise was from other streams and tributaries and the recent rainstorms. This high water would have a big impact on what we saw (or didn't see), because there was little dry land for alligators to haul themselves out onto. Near the end of the trip, Beanie pushed the nose of the boat into some of the tall vegetation where he knew an alligator had a nest. Sure

enough, we got to see three of the babies—each about twelve inches long, with a brown-and-yellow banded pattern to help camouflage them.

Most of the passengers were hoping to see alligators, but we were happy just being out on the water and seeing new habitat. Somebody spotted a small water snake of some sort swimming away from the boat. Beanie said when he was a kid there were lots of snakes on this river, but now he hardly sees any. We sighted an osprey flying off to the left and Beanie let us know we'd be passing by several nests. The next one we saw was perched in a tree close to the water with a fish under one foot. It wasn't comfortable with us coming so close so it took off and found a better spot to have its meal. Several old osprey nests balanced precariously at the top of some dead trees, but the most interesting one was built on the top of a tree that had tilted out over the river, so that it was only ten feet above the stream. We had never seen an osprey nest so low. There was one adult in the nest and another perched in a nearby tree.

The most disturbing news Beanie shared with us had to do with the marsh wrens. He told us there used to be thousands of these small, melodic birds and their compact little nests built on the leaves of the grasses, but since Katrina there are none, even though the plants are still there. No one seems to have an answer for their disappearance.

Our boat trip would take us into backwater *bayous* (another Choctaw word, meaning "slow-moving water"). One was called Whiskey Bayou and he said there might still be some stills back in there. He told us to keep our eyes out for wild hogs, which are a serious invasive species. Even with a hunting season, they can't get them under control. The hogs really create havoc with the vegetation in the marsh.

Coming back onto the river we were shown a place where it has changed directions, post-Katrina. The storm took down a bunch of trees and gradually the land has been eroded away, taking the river in a new direction. This is what rivers do when they are not under the influence of humans.

The Pascagoula River is unique, as it's the only river of its size in the Gulf drainage that is still a natural unaffected basin, unlike the Mississippi. The Nature Conservancy says, "The Pascagoula River is the largest (by volume) unimpeded river system in the contiguous forty-eight states." We cannot attest to this, but we understand why so many people are trying to protect it. It is also called the Singing River, about which the Nature Conservancy explains, "According to legend, the peace-loving Pascagoula Indian tribe sang as they walked hand-in-hand into the river to avoid fighting with the invading Biloxi tribe. It is said that on quiet nights you can still hear them singing their death chant."

This is a canoeing river, a fishing river, a hunting river, a source of nutrients to the shrimp fisheries, and a treasure, but as such it is vulnerable. A recent threat to divert millions of gallons a day into a salt dome for the storage of oil would have harmed the river and diverted such salty water into the Gulf that another dead zone would form. It was defeated once, but such threats do not go away.

We returned to the dock near the Audubon Center's office and thanked our knowledgeable guide for the introduction to his world. Then it was back on the road toward New Orleans, where we had lunch at Nonna Mia's Café and Pizzeria in a neighborhood called Mid-City. The neighborhood had narrow streets with wooden-sided houses placed close to one another, and the restaurant itself was an old home converted into an eating establishment. In the pleasantly warm, but not too humid, weather we sat on the brick patio, where Mike ordered and enjoyed a margherita pizza, and I had lobster ravioli, which was also excellent. Looking around us, it was hard to tell that six years earlier this city was inundated by flood waters. There were still places boarded up and empty, but others seemed to have either escaped the worst of the water damage or managed to rebound quickly.

March 28
New Orleans, Louisiana, to Natchez, Mississippi

OUR FIRST DECISION was to have breakfast at The Broken Egg, located in Mandeville, Louisiana. The reviews proclaimed it had some of the best omelets and southern specialty dishes. However, not knowing the area very well, we didn't realize that Mandeville was twenty-six miles away— across Lake Ponchartrain, the second-largest inland body of saltwater in the United States, after the Great Salt Lake in Utah.

Like Nonna Mia's Café, The Broken Egg is located in an old home, with various rooms converted to dining spaces. Many of the reviews we'd read said that service had been slow and less than friendly, but the food was highly recommended. We arrived around 8:00 A.M. on a Wednesday, which was a good thing because it was not crowded. Even so, we did find only a few servers working and people did have to wait a while for their food. We reminded ourselves, "This is the south, and we're all just so impatient nowadays." The food was worth the wait. Mike had the Hey Ricky omelet, which had avocado, cheese, salsa, and chorizo cooked within it. Fried potatoes and English muffins accompanied his entrée. It was a lot of food, but he ate it all. I had something called the Southern Stack, which included a crab cake placed upon a mound of grits and covered in a rich sauce with shrimp and Andouille sausage. It was spicy and delicious, but too rich. I only ate half of it and took the rest along to finish the next morning.

It was seventy-nine degrees and humid when we left. The levees prevented us from seeing the actual river, but it appeared as though a bicyclist could ride on top of them for much of the way. This was our big question, as so much of this southern portion of the river has levees next to the road and they appear to be perfect for bikers. Later, when we crossed the river at Reserve to Edgarton on the ferry, we started seeing signs all along the levees saying PRIVATE PROPERTY NO TRESPASSING, with $100 fines for those caught on them. It appeared by the signage this was from a law passed in 2011. A phone number was listed for the Atchafalaya Basin Levee District and Mike called to ask about the actual rules and possibility of getting permission to ride on them. The woman informed us that all of the levees are owned by different people, and we'd have to get permission from each one—a logistic impossibility. It's really a shame if non-motorized recreationists cannot access these surfaces. They are a hell of a lot safer than the roadways.

Before taking the car ferry across the river we drove through a region that can only be called Cancer Alley or Chemical Alley. Massive refineries (Shell) and chemical (DuPont) plants line either side of the river, their

twisting steel pipes and tall stacks spreading across the horizon. The river here is not what we would consider boater-friendly, as massive ocean-going oil carriers and tugs pushing twenty to forty barges each vie for room to pass. A canoe or kayak would be dwarfed and easily swamped by these massive ships, though we know people have canoed and kayaked the river down to the Gulf of Mexico.

This is a region of old plantations, and the road took us past many of the stately buildings, some of which have been restored and opened to the public for tours. Near these homes we found the most massive and stately live oaks, wearing their long shawls of Spanish moss. Parula warblers use the Spanish moss in their nests. In the north, these warblers use Old Man's Beard—Usnia—to make their nests. The two plants resemble one another, although the Spanish moss is a flowering plant and Usnia is a lichen, but both work well for the Parulas. Some of these oak trees are well over 400 years old. Their impressive shape stems from a short main trunk with many long and thick branches. Some of the branches reach far beyond the trunk—almost the length that the tree is tall—bending down to touch the ground like the flying buttresses used in so many cathedrals around the world.

The best bird of the day was a fork-tailed kite I saw fly over the road. Mike grumbled, not having seen it. Along this stretch of road up to and beyond Plaquemine, Louisiana, we started seeing signs along the side of the road that said WATER PROTECTION AREA. We were very curious to learn what that meant. The Department of Environmental Quality (DEQ) says,

> A Source Water Protection Area defines the zone through which contaminants, if present, are likely to migrate and reach a drinking water well or surface water intake. Every public water system obtains its water from either a ground water source (aquifer) or a surface water source (stream, river, reservoir or lake). Delineation of source water protection areas is based on the source of the water supply.

Weaving our way along a road on top of a stretch of levee, we encountered the Old River Control Complex. This is the place where the Mississippi River is connected to the Atchafalaya River and other backwaters and where many of the dams work to remove water from the Mississippi when it is too high for safe navigation. A series of sluices and dam-like structures have been built to control just how much water the Mississippi

will be allowed to send this way. Author John McPhee describes this human endeavor extremely well in his book *The Control of Nature*. We recommend it to everyone, regardless of your interest in the river—it is very well written and insightful.

Our goal was to reach Natchez, a beautiful town built on a bluff above the river. We found lodging at a casino hotel, where the actual casino is several blocks away on a paddlewheel tied up to the shore in an area known as "Natchez Under the Hill." This area has a long history of riverboat transportation. It was here that floating brothels, gambling boats, and hooligans gathered, ready to rob travelers coming down the river. It was the busiest anchorage on the river for many years. Natchez brought together such names as Jim Bowie, Andrew Jackson, John James Audubon, Merriwether Lewis, Aaron Burr, and General Wilkinson, among many others.

We had heard about Fat Mama's Tamales restaurant and found it just a few blocks away. Before this trip, we did not know how popular tamales were in these southern states, but they are. Oh, and they usually serve them with saltine crackers. We ordered half a dozen at this popular location, along with their Get Naked Margaritas. Sitting on the patio in the warm late afternoon air was a pleasant change from the long hours in the car.

March 29
Natchez, Mississippi, to Holly Springs and Strawberry Plains Audubon Center

THE AIR HAD A HAZE of humidity in the morning, but the temperature was a pleasant seventy degrees. I suggested we walk down to the "Natchez Under the Hill" area before we started driving.

Our hotel was on a busy street and before we crossed I spotted a small, brown-brindled dog walking toward us. He seemed friendly enough, as he trotted next to and ahead of us. When I went to pet him, he rolled over onto his back in submission, and I rubbed his belly as he blissfully licked his lips. After we started walking again, I thought, *Oh, boy, I probably own him now.* He was such a happy-go-lucky fellow I decided that if he had a name, it would be Happy Jack Brindle.

We walked down a sidewalk past some abandoned houses perched higher up on a slope. Cement steps and railings still led up to empty lots. It seemed like prime real estate, since they are up on the bluff looking down on the river. On the corner was a very old and rotting log house. Happy Jack strayed behind us, sniffing at interesting spots, and then trotted ahead. He crossed the street before us as we all walked down the steep hill toward the river. Stopping occasionally, he would look back at us and wait for us to catch up.

It was early enough in the morning that none of the establishments were open on the waterfront, but the cliff swallows were noisily flying in squadrons above the water. The day before when we drove past the paddlewheel, we could see them swooping under the gangplank hoisted out over the river. It's either a good place to build nests or there are lots of insects underneath it. The other birds we heard this morning were cardinals, mockingbirds, and tufted titmice.

We made a loop, climbing back up to the bluff on a sidewalk matching the one we came down. Sirens in the distance caused Happy Jack to stop and peer over his shoulder with his ears cocked upward. This happened several times, and we wondered what experiences he'd had with emergency vehicles. At the top of the bluff where there was a park of sorts, he ran ahead, and we took a turn to the right, thinking maybe he would forget about us. Soon we heard the telltale click of nails on the sidewalk behind us, and then he was passing us with a doggy grin spread across his muzzle.

We really worried about him as we neared the busy street. At an intersection where there was a stop light, he started to go out and we yelled at him to get back on the curb, which he did. A bus driver crossed the street and asked, "Is that your dog?" We said, "No." She replied, "I saw him earlier. He must be a stray."

When we crossed the street, Happy Jack turned the corner back toward the river, where up on the bluff there was an old mansion open to the public. We could see people going into it and it was where the woman we'd spoken to was headed. The dog glanced back over his shoulder once, but apparently decided we were not going where he wanted to go (thankfully). And so we left our little Natchez guide behind, hoping he would somehow manage to survive the busy streets around him.

We drove north through a winding, deep forest filled with birdsong and no shoulders at all, heading for the Natchez Trace Parkway. It was along this stretch of road that we heard the first blue jay since we'd entered the true south. A red-bellied woodpecker also called out. The parkway is a perfectly smooth, fairly quiet roadway, with forests on either side. Wild turkeys skipped across the road, and twice we stopped to rescue three-toed box turtles slowly trying to get across. These were plainer looking than the ornate box turtle we had moved in Kentucky.

The trace angled northeast, but I wanted to revisit a place we found a few years ago along this route, the Mississippi Arts and Crafts Center. It had the most magnificent, diverse collection of handmade arts and crafts of the region. Last time I found a ruby-colored gourd and could only afford one, but hoped they might still have some to add to my collection. The center, located north of Jackson, was not in the direction we really needed to go, but Mike was willing to humor me. Naturally, they no longer carried those gourds. They said the people stopped making them, but she did find one similar to the originals, shaped like an apple and a deep, red mahogany.

Around 4:30 P.M., we pulled into the town of Holly Springs, described by one publication as an antebellum encyclopedia. Home to the Finley family, who donated the home and land, it was now the Strawberry Plains Audubon Center. The environmental center was one Mike consulted on when it was first accepted by Audubon.

The town square was surrounded by a business district that had seen better times. We were able to picture it in our minds in those days as a bustling, thriving community, but one that would have been segregated and beset by more problems than poverty.

The magnificent plantation house, which was restored in the 1970s, would be our lodging for the night. Many of the furnishings were antiques that belonged to the original owners, who built the house in 1850. We were the only people in the house that night, and I wondered about ghosts in a place with such a long and tumultuous history.

Originally a cotton plantation, during the Civil War, the mistress of the house shot and killed a Yankee soldier on the steps leading to the second floor. The soldiers burned the house in retaliation. The brick shell remained, and members of the family managed to live there afterward, repairing what they could. This was actually the "farm" for the Finleys, who had an equally grand house in town.

March 30
Strawberry Plains

BEFORE HITTING THE ROAD, we met with Bubba Hubbard, the director of the Audubon Center, Andrea Schuhmann, their outreach person, and Chad Pope, the center ecologist. We appreciated these local resources and the networks they could link us up with. Andrea, an avid biker and originally from Kentucky, said she had found the ethic in Mississippi very different

than what she was used to. She didn't want to scare us, but wanted us to know that there wasn't a lot of respect on the road for people riding bikes.

A couple features of Strawberry Plains that we really liked were the rain chains and the chimney swift houses. On the back porches of houses, from each of the downspouts was a metal rain chain. Each was different and all were works of art—literally—made by local metal workers. A favorite looked like a string of dreamcatchers, but when looking closer, each one had a realistic looking spider (its body a stone wrapped in metal) in the middle. I have always loved singing "Itsy-Bitsy Spider" with the grandkids, and here was a perfect illustration. There were several of the chimney swift houses like we'd seen at the Pascagoula River Center. The chimney swifts were just starting to return to this area and soon would be streaming into these fake chimneys each evening. We saw one or two flying overhead as we loaded our car.

We decided to backtrack to Greenville, Mississippi, to get back on the MRT bike trail and find places listed in *Feasting On Asphalt*. The Spanish moss no longer draped from the trees. Instead, we saw acres of dead kudzu draped over shrubs and plants like vast brown netting. It appears to have engulfed parts of the landscape. Black vultures hunched on branches of dead-looking trees or clustered on the road around unidentifiable carcasses.

As we entered the community of Leland, Mississippi, we saw a sign announcing the birthplace of Kermit the Frog! Then there was the sign pointing to the museum. How could we pass it by? Turning at the next corner, we circled around the block and came up in front of a small wooden building perched above Dream Creek, Kermit's birthplace according to Jim Henson. We went inside and were met by a friendly elderly lady by the name of Dot, who was a font of information when it came to Jim Henson's history. Display cases held various Muppets, and Kermit was in a place of prominence. Jane

Henson, Jim's widow, provided many of the photos and artifacts and some financial support over the years. We couldn't leave without patronizing the little gift store and contributing by buying a DVD and book.

Dot Turk was a wonderfully vivacious woman who was pleased to see us and loved to share stories about Jim Henson. One story began, "When he was four years old, he did a scrapbook of bird pictures and then he began to draw birds." Pointing to a photograph, Dot continued, "This is his grandmother, who he called 'Dear.' Her name was Sarah Brown. She was an artist and he got his artistic ability from her. She was also a nature lover and she had a great sense of humor. They were two peas in a pod.

"When he was five, he came in and said, 'Dear, I need to go to school now.' She questioned that, and he kept insisting I 'need to go now.' She finally said, 'Okay, Jimmy, why do you need to go now?' [He answered,] 'Because I need to know how to write my name so I can sign my artwork.'"

Showing us a photograph, she said, "This is his scout troop, troop number forty-two." In the troop with Jim were his brother Paul and many friends. Pointing to one, Dot said,

This particular friend remained a friend all of Jim's life, and they talked just before Jim died. Jane loved his name. She said it was the most southern name she ever heard. His name is Royall Fraser, and Royall has two "L"s on it.

The friend who is not in this picture is Kermit Scott, and Kermit Scott was one of his school friends at the elementary school who grew up to be a professor of philosophy at Purdue University. He didn't know the frog was named for him until after the movie came out. After the movie came out, the *New York Times* magazine came out with a special edition of "Muppets Go to Movieland," and in it Jim talked about how he loved names, like when he was a child if you asked him what his favorite bird was he would say it was the purple crackle, and he also liked names of things, like his friend Kermit Scott. So the newspaper sent a copy of that to Kermit, and here is Kermit as he finds out from this magazine that he was honored by a frog.

Deer Creek is where, as you can see here, Jim writes to Leland is the birthplace of the frog. Deer Creek was his favorite place to play. That's where he got his pets, and he would bring home turtles and snakes and frogs. And Dear said that he was pretty good at keeping them outside but it still paid to look before you sat.

This is Jim when he was in fifth grade. I had a little boy in here a while ago and I took him out and showed him the school and he said, "Wonderful, then Kermit could hop over there and play with him at recess."

When Jim proposed [to Jane], he looked like the picture over there with Ed Sullivan [where Jim sported a full beard]. Jane didn't care, but his mother did. She just had a fit. The very idea of her son getting married looking like that! So she went to Jane and she said, "Jane, he won't

listen to me and you know it and I know it, but you know you can do it: get the beard off the man." She did a very good job of it and when she got back from the honeymoon there was a box waiting for her. Inside the box was the beard with a note—"From Samson to Delilah."

He didn't intend to be an entertainer—he was going to be an artist—but he went to all of the stations in Washington asking for jobs as an artist. None of them had anything, but as he was leaving a WRC which was in D.C., he saw a notice on the bulletin board that they needed a puppeteer for a children show. It didn't last very long, so he decided he would do his own, which he named *Sam and Friends*. His program was not for children. [Sam was a human-like bald puppet with friends Yorick the Hipster, Professor Madcliffe, Chicken Liver, and a lizard-like puppet called Kermit.] It came on at 10:25 at night and it was a satire on the radio. Edward R. Murrow was the most famous person at the time. He was a chain smoker and he had a show, *Person to Person*, and he smoked all the time on the show. Jim had a Muppet, Ed Murrow, who had a cigarette hanging out its mouth. His program was *Poison to Poison*.

Jim decided he wanted money to buy cars—plural! This wouldn't do it—he got five dollars every time one of the five-minute episodes would air. So he decided to do TV commercials. He did 160 commercials, which must have done it because he drove up to graduation in a Rolls Royce that he paid cash for. Those commercials were responsible for getting him into show business, because one of those commercials was a Purina Dog Chow commercial. Jimmy Dean had a variety show then. He saw that commercial and he called Jim and said, "I really liked that dog. Will you come and be a regular on my show, which is being shown nationally?" That was his first national exposure.

He readily did that and that dog turned out to be Rowlf the Dog. He had to take Frank Oz with him because Frank was Rowlf the Dog. He [Frank] ended up doing a little bit of everything, and he created Miss Piggy, which he called his warped idea of womanhood.

Those two were so talented that they had a really hard time following the script. Frank's favorite story is about a script that came through where Miss Piggy was supposed to slap Kermy. Well, Frank didn't feel like it that day, so he just did a karate chop instead.

Dot would have been happy to entertain us with stories for another hour, but we needed to be on our way.

In Greenville, Mississippi, we were looking for honest-to-goodness Mississippi Hot Tamales at Doe's Eat Place. But Mike's mouth was watering for steak, which was also advertised when we stepped through the door of a tiny, white-sided building. An African-American woman was standing at a stove, hovering over some very large saucepans. A couple other ladies had come in before us and were picking up tamales to go, which we found out was all we could buy at this time of day. We ordered a dozen and the owner put them into a foam container for us. Then she grabbed a handful of saltine cracker packages and stuck them in the container.

I asked how they're supposed to accompany the tamales. She said she had no idea; that was just what people want. Personally, we didn't find the crackers improving the taste or texture of the tamales. We took them with us and found a picnic table at Winterville Mounds State Park, believed to have been a ceremonial site in 1000 C.E. for early Indian cultures known as the mound builders. Cahokia was not the only site for mounds—they are found throughout the lower Mississippi River and Ohio River valleys.

The belief is that the mounds culture prospered for 5,000 years and would have met early Spanish explorers. Over 2,500 sites have been found, but why they stopped building could be the result of drought, disease, or some unknown forces.

Our next stop was the town of Rosedale (also on the bike route) at the White Front Café, where we hoped to find Koolickles. *Feasting on Asphalt* described them as pickles made with Kool-Aid. We were hoping to bring a jar back to our neighbor. It was another small, white-sided building on the main street, but inside it had a few tables and looked more like a little café. We were disappointed again when

the owner, Miss Barbara, said she had no koolickles available. She did have tamales, though—so we bought six more. These were better than the ones from Doe's, plus they were wrapped in corn husks.

Here Mike expressed his surprise at finding tamales all over the delta. The woman looked up at him and said, "Where else have you found them?" Mike explained that he thought of them as coming from Arizona, New Mexico, and Mexico. She looked stunned and said, "Do they have them there, too?" It's all in your perspective.

As we continued up Highway 1, we could see the levee off to our left across and past flat farm fields. Crossing a bridge into Arkansas from Mississippi, the road took us onto Crowley's Ridge Parkway! Mike saw the sign and stopped so we could walk back and take a photo of me beneath it. The bridge itself is very busy and there is no bike lane, so we will require a ride across when the time comes.

Arriving in Helena, Arkansas, we stopped to look at signage on the levee that talked about the Memorial to the Trail of Tears—another sad chapter in American history when the Native American tribes of the southeast were taken from their homes and land and marched (and loaded onto flatboats towed behind paddlewheels) through Arkansas and over to Oklahoma. Thousands died along the way.

We followed the Great River Road out of town. It took us past an old cemetery, the sign of which said Confederate Cemetery. Next to it were two fenced-in cemeteries—one for the Catholics and one for the Jews. Suddenly the asphalt ran out, and we were on a dirt road. This didn't seem right, but we continued to follow it. This was part of a national forest and wildlife refuge, and we weren't sure where we'd come out, but the GPS showed some other roads entering up ahead. In the forest, tufted titmice and blue jays called out. After this unexpected "shortcut," our poor little Prius was very much in need of a bath.

March 31
Memphis, Tennessee

It was a sunny day, even though thunderstorms were predicted, and it was warm and humid when we left at 10:00 a.m. to go to Mud Island, where we hoped to rent bikes. However, we discovered they don't open until the second weekend in April.

Mud Island is actually a peninsula and includes a very large greenway park. In fact, we counted twenty bike riders in less than one hour, more than we'd seen during the entire trip. We could hear purple martins calling overhead and were sorry that there were no purple martin houses of any kind on this parkland. It was ideal habitat.

After walking up and down the parkway in the hot sunshine, we were ready to find a cool place to have lunch. Neither one of us had ever been to Beale Street, so that's where we went next. The first place we saw was B.B. King's Club and, since he was one of our favorite musicians, that was where we went. Mike ordered ribs—what else—and I got a pulled pork sandwich. The walls of the darkened club (not smoky, thankfully) were covered with framed and autographed guitars, as well as photos and other memorabilia. Best yet, a group got up on stage while we were still eating and proceeded to sing and play the blues, while the audience clapped their hands and shimmied in their seats.

The temperature by this time had reached the high eighties, and it was uncomfortable to be without shade, so we finished walking up Beale Street and headed to the Peabody Hotel, an institution that came up with a clever PR scheme seventy-five years ago. Five mallard ducks come down on an elevator every morning with their red-coated, gold-epaulette-laden handler and parade down the hallway until they reach a fountain in the main lobby. Then they climb up and splash into the little pool, where they spend the day paddling and eating. At 5:00 P.M., they hop out of the pool and reverse their route back upstairs. People come in droves to observe the brief ceremony and special retinue.

Memphis had a wonderful old-fashioned electric trolley system that ran up and down the main street and also made a loop along the river frontage. Like many towns, it got rid of its original system and had to turn elsewhere for trolleys. In this case there were three sources—some trolleys came from Portugal, following the Brill design of the two historic U.S. Brill trolleys, and seven more were from Melbourne, Australia, while additional cars had been built in the last few years by Gomaco using "Birney" designs. The original trolleys were pulled by mules. We climbed aboard and sat on a too-small wooden seat, with warm air pouring in the open window. You know people were smaller in the "olden" days by the size of the seats. Mike's right leg was partway out into the narrow aisle, so he finally moved up to the front part of the car.

The car trundled down the street past well-kept older buildings and others that have seen better times. The return portion of the loop took us behind some huge homes facing the river. One didn't need to be a child to enjoy a trolley ride, though we did wish we had our grandkids with us. A year

after our visit, the city closed down the trolleys, and they have not reopened. The town hopes to get new trolleys, however, and to restart the service.

One of the more striking buildings in town is a full-size pyramid—the sixth-largest pyramid in the world, a fact that did not impress us. It was originally used as a basketball stadium for the Memphis Grizzlies and now the stainless steel structure will hold a Bass Pro Shop. We looked at this massive structure with the hot sun bouncing off all sides and thought, *Why don't they have solar panels all over it?!* In this area of Egyptian names—Cairo to Memphis—it was probably appropriate, but what we were told was that it was Memphis's answer to the Nashville Parthenon.

For dinner that night we drove to Colliersville to eat at the Mexican restaurant, El Porton. We were very happy with our meal, especially the "made at your table" guacamole. Colliersville was advertised as a small town with a historic square I wanted to see. It also expanded into a very prosperous-looking suburb, with lots of the usual outlying shopping malls. We found the old square, a wooded island with masses of blooming azaleas. It was after 6:00 P.M., which was a good thing because all the shops were closed, and all I could do was put my face to the windows. An old train was parked on tracks on one side of the square, being used as a backdrop for wedding pictures as we walked by.

April 1
Memphis, Tennessee, to St. Louis, Missouri

IT WAS SEVENTY-NINE DEGREES without a cloud in the sky as we left Memphis in the morning. The MRT bike route follows the greenway and then winds through neighborhoods, past a cypress swamp full of "knees."

We passed two bikers with flashing red lights on the backs of their bikes and thought about stopping to talk to them, but didn't. After turning onto a busier road, we stopped a short way up so Mike could take some photos of the cypress swamp. That's when the two bikers caught up with us and Mike flagged them down to talk. The couple from Memphis had mapped a route south of the city. The man told us they were headed to the Shelby Forest General Store. We didn't realize our route would take us to the same spot.

While we stood talking to them, bicycle riders—singly and in groups—passed on both sides of the highway. Memphis appeared to be a very bicycle-oriented town, at least compared to the other cities we'd visited.

The Shelby Forest General Store is an old wooden building on a corner of a rural intersection. When we drove past, it had just been filled up by a horde of motorcyclists. As we slowly turned the corner we saw written on the wall of the store, WORLD FAMOUS CHEESEBURGERS. Since it was lunch time we decided to stop—they also advertised fried bologna and turkey melts.

The inside of the store was filled with people standing in front of the counter; animal trophy heads, antlers, and snake skins hung on the walls and draped over the exposed beams; and behind the counter three women worked feverishly at a grill. A very loud and talkative man was handling the cash register. When we checked out to pay, we reminded him that we had ordered sodas. "Sodas!" he exclaimed. "Where are you from?" We told him Minnesota, and that we could have said "pop." He laughed at that, too.

When we asked what they call them "down here," he said, "we call everything a 'Coke.' You could order a can of root beer and we'd say 'Coke.'" Now it was our turn to laugh, but he joined in.

One of the women behind the counter thanked us several times for our patience. The motorcycle club had

arrived en masse, and they had thirty orders to fill. We sat at the counter reading newspapers while we waited for our world famous cheeseburgers. They were good ones, and the atmosphere and clientele in the store was worth the stop.

We talked about the heat with the proprietor when we left, and he said they'd broken a record the day before and were due to break it again today.

The next road we took was two lanes, curvy, and rural. Suddenly up ahead on the road we saw an animal trotting toward us. At first we assumed it was a dog, then we saw that it was all white. I said "fox," (the farm-raised kind), but Mike said, "No, that's a raccoon." And so it was. We slowed down, but the raccoon veered into the woods. Mike jumped out of the car and ran in pursuit with his camera, but the little white bandit disappeared. Neither one of us had ever seen an albino raccoon.

We were very appreciative of the MRT signs when they were in place, but we found them missing at some critical junctures, which ended up sending us in circles. We tried to follow the written directions in the MRT guidebook, but they were not always helpful, either.

By 2:15 P.M., it was eighty-five degrees and puffy clouds floated overhead. At 4:15, it had reached ninety. Mother Nature's April Fool's joke on us humans.

We reached St. Louis around 6:30 and drove to our hotel, a Hyatt located just across the street from the Gateway Arch. Our room had a fabulous view looking toward the arch and the river beyond. They had designed the hotel so most rooms had this perspective.

John Oehler, one of our Lake Superior Voyageur Canoe companions, had driven over from Cincinnati to join us for the evening so he and Mike could sample bourbons, a shared interest they discovered during the canoe trip.

April 2
St. Louis, Missouri

OUR FIRST FULL DAY in St. Louis dawned clear but hazy with humidity and the promise of heat. It reached a record-breaking ninety degrees by 2:45 that afternoon. The arch was overhead in all of its reflective glory as we walked up the steep steps back to our hotel. I was imagining his massive monument covered in solar panels. Just like the Pyramid in Memphis, it could be creating so much energy, symbolizing another kind of gateway to the future.

Our next goal was to find a laundromat, so we turned down a side street and in the process discovered the Billy Goat Chip Company. It was a small brick building, and our curiosity was piqued by the name. We parked the car and walked in the door wondering what kinds of chips they made—computer, chocolate? As soon as we stepped inside, we saw the potato chips in bags and bins. It's an interesting story of entrepreneurship and local products. The chips were originally made and served in a St. Louis restaurant, but became so popular that the owner closed the restaurant, opened this mini-factory, and began selling the chips all over the city. They didn't sell them at this location but a worker told us there was a deli "within walking distance" where we could buy some. He gave us directions, and we started out. After five blocks and no deli in sight, we began to wonder what his idea of "walking distance" was. Obviously we have no reservations about walking, but the air was heating up and we didn't know how far we might have to go, so we decided to turn back to the car.

On the way, we passed a building that said LINK CHIROPRACTIC. Mike couldn't resist and went inside and explained to the receptionist his reason for coming in. One branch of his Link ancestors settled in and around St. Louis. Mike wondered whether he could talk to the doctor. I went on to get the car and when I returned, Mike was sitting in the lobby talking to another

man. A bike enthusiast, Dr. Daniel Link gave Mike some brochures about biking in the St. Louis area. It was a fortuitous meeting and who knows, it could potentially add some more information to Mike's family history.

We drove on, still looking for the deli. Neither of us had ever driven through the neighborhoods of St. Louis, but on this trip we were amazed to find that nearly every house in the town (at least the older neighborhoods) seemed to be made of brick.

We found a laundromat and Mike dropped me off. A half hour later he returned, triumphant and excited, having found the Macklind Avenue Deli. We went back to the store so he could show why he was so impressed. It was filled with a variety of beer, wines, and sodas. It did have a display case filled with more traditional deli foods, as well as the Billy Goat chips, but it was the beverages Mike was most happy to find. The trunk of our car was filling up with an assortment of liquid treats Mike intended to sample with his buddies Bill and Dick back home.

I went back to the hotel and to work on the computer while Mike went out in search of a bike station. Downtown St. Louis has done much to promote and help foster bike commuting by creating "stations" where people can park their bikes while at work. They even have showers for bikers to use. The one he found was connected to a bike shop that sold and rented bikes.

Later we drove to the Dogtown neighborhood where we had an early dinner at Las Gras Italian Tapas and Wine Bar. We shared a plate of

bruschetta and a sampler plate of tapas. Sitting at a table out on the sidewalk we listened to but didn't understand the conversation of three Russian girls. Laughter and excited chatter are the universal language of young adulthood.

The next day, the sky was overcast, and thunderstorms were in the forecast. It was already seventy-eight degrees when we left our hotel to walk to the Big Shark bike shop/bike station eight blocks away. Downtown St. Louis is a lively place during the daytime hours. The architecture is a mix of new and old skyscrapers, and we enjoyed gawking at the details on the older buildings.

We rented two hybrid commuting style bikes and set off on our exploration of the River Trail that the city has paved close to the river's edge. However, the river just north of the downtown area is highly industrialized, so it wasn't exactly a bucolic ride. One of the sites we passed was *Lorax*-looking with huge piles of scrap metal, including whole, crushed cars, tires and all. Clanking cranes grabbed pieces in their metal claws and dropped them onto a conveyor belt that emptied into an enclosed structure. At the other end, a pile of brown material grew into a cone. Smoke rose from stacks, while grinding and crashing sounds filled the air. On the other side of the trail, barges disgorged materials into pipes that crossed overhead, and trucks rumbled in and out of walled off work sites. Dust swirled behind them. Freight trains filled two or three tracks to our left. A tent and lean-to camp of the homeless was built next to one of the work areas.

And yet, close to the river where trees, shrubs, and grass were allowed to grow, wildlife flourished. We saw a wild tom turkey displaying proudly to three uninterested hens as they picked their way through the grass. A red-tailed hawk circled down and landed on the crossbars of a transmission tower. Red-winged blackbirds called to one another from either side, robins flew into the undergrowth, and a killdeer swooped up suddenly from a rocky bit of ground that could well have held its nest. Nature is tenacious, but we couldn't help but wonder just how much waste, toxic or otherwise, was ending up in the river that continued to flow with determination to the south. We rode for an hour and then turned back to retrace our route, going further past the arch and looping through the streets of the business district, back to the Big Shark bike shop.

Hungry after our ride, we stopped at a very busy and popular grocery store right in the center of the downtown. Called Schnuks Market/Culinaria, it was a delightful oasis of fresh produce and a wide selection of deli food, both hot and cold. Every city should be

so lucky to have such a quality grocery store for people living in the heart of the city, or even those who work there. We found people of all economic levels enjoying the shopping and eating al fresco at the sidewalk tables out front. Mike bought pizza and I had a delicious "handmade" salad.

We had a 2:00 P.M. appointment scheduled at the Riverlands Audubon Center north of the city where Patty Hagen was the director of the center, which was leased from the Army Corps of Engineers. The building had some great displays of wetland ecology and they were working to provide programs for the public focused on the river and its environs.

This center is located very close to the confluence of the Mississippi and Missouri rivers. A state park protects this nationally significant location, and we couldn't leave without seeing it. A gravel path wound up from a parking lot and we walked beside the fast-moving Missouri River. Unseen blackbirds filled the nearby forest with raucous calls; otherwise we only heard the sound of the wind through the trees and the water moving against the shoreline. The path came to an end at the point (literally) where the two great rivers merge.

At ground level we could not see the mixing of the waters—one typically brown and the other navy blue by comparison. I took off my sandals and stood in some shallow water, effectively baptizing them in this ancient mixture. A silty, muddy layer coated the bottom of my feet when I stepped out, a graphic example of what is being carried by these rivers as they go south to the gulf.

There was an elevation marker on the point that read 406 FEET—we were 1,000 feet below the headwaters and only 406 above the Gulf of Mexico. Further up the path we encountered a tall pole with the information that high water of thirty-eight feet above normal was reached at this spot in 1993. Bending our necks back, we looked up to the upper branches of the trees and imagined water filling all that space. It was hard to comprehend such a flood, but there is no question it happened in the past and will happen again in the future. It's hard for us humans to believe something so elemental, something critical for our survival could also have so much strength that we are powerless in the face of its ferocity. It's humbling, to say the least.

As we left the park we encountered a slider (a type of turtle) and though it was probably okay on this nearly deserted gravel road, habit made us stop, get out, and move it to the side, after Mike took its picture.

That night we found one of the best restaurants of the trip—Square One Brewery and Distillery. It was in the LaFayette Square neighborhood of St. Louis, an area that seems to be a mix of gentrification and decay. We hope rehabilitation will include people of all economic levels.

Mike was in heaven at Square One. They distill their own whiskey, vodka, tequila, absinthe, rum, and make great beers and burgers, too. It was burger night, so what else could we ask for?

April 3
St. Louis, Missouri, to Keokuk, Iowa

WE LEFT ST. LOUIS with low, overcast skies and the temperature at seventy-three degrees. Within a half-hour it had dropped to a cool sixty-three degrees. We were headed for Dreamland Palace, a German-themed restaurant in Foster Pond, Illinois. The salad bar alone made us happy. Mike was thrilled because, "there aren't any green leafy things." Instead there was an assortment of pickled salads (carrot, cabbage, tomato, and green bean). The menu included many well-known German entrées. Mike settled on the *sauerbraten* and I had the *roulade*, a slice of beef rolled around a pickle. Their potato pancakes were the best. They resembled big, flat hashbrown patties, more than a pancake. Red cabbage and applesauce accompanied the dishes. Both of us have German ancestry, and it is expressed in our love of this cuisine.

After our filling lunch, we retraced our route back to St. Louis and then began our drive north to Hannibal on a busy two-lane highway with a wide shoulder. After passing the town of Clarksville (The Monkees' *Last Train to Clarksville* song played in our heads), the road ran right next to the river, which was a welcome change. Here is one chorus so it can get into your head, too:

Take the last train to Clarksville.
I'll be waiting at the station.
We'll have time for coffee flavored kisses
And a bit of conversation.
Oh . . . Oh, no, no, no!
Oh, no, no, no!

Louisiana, Missouri, is situated on high bluffs that gave us a broad, sweeping view of the river and its valley. A bridge crosses the river here into Illinois. The Champ Clark bridge is 2,238.4 feet with a span over the main channel of the Mississippi 418.5 feet in length Even on a cloudy day, it was a beautiful sight.

Hannibal is of course a very famous and historic river town, the childhood home of Samuel Clemens/Mark Twain. We last came through here in 1991 with our kids on our way south to the Okefenokee Swamp. The town has classic late-nineteenth-century two-story buildings on the main street, with decorative, elaborate trim painted in contrasting colors. It appears that parts of the town are still doing well, especially during the summer and fall seasons. It was raining slightly when we came through, and it gave the town a more sober, somber appearance, but if we listened

closely we could still imagine the calliope music from a long ago paddlewheeler drifting on the breeze. We paid our respects to the Huck and Tom statue and moved on.

April 4
Highway 61 and the Lincoln Highway

CATHY WURZER, RADIO HOST on Minnesota Public Radio, wrote the book on Highway 61 in Minnesota and brought back nostalgia for this north/south highway. It is fascinating, and we thought a lot about it as we traveled so much of it on our way to the Gulf of Mexico. Perhaps it should be known as the Mississippi Highway.

In Galena, Illinois, we walked among the brick buildings, bought spices and pickles at the Garlic Shop, a pie cover at the Gourmet Shop, salsa and hot sauce at another specialty store, and picked up a mixed six-pack of root beer at a root beer store. Really—a root beer store! We shared a root beer float before heading back to the car. The local economy definitely benefitted with this stop—not our plan originally, but that's how it goes on road trips.

Picking up Highway 61 in East Dubuque, we traveled north to Dickeyville, Wisconsin. We found this hilarious and some will think that irreverent, but we enjoy the trappings of religion and all the unique ways people find to express their faith (as long as they are not forcing their beliefs or harming others). The Holy Ghost Park and Grotto on the Wisconsin Heritage Trail looks like someone spent a lifetime building structures, fences, towers and monuments with colored stones, glass, and seashells. It was a holy version of the Kinderhook Post Office.

Along this stretch was in the town of Tennyson. We wondered if people there read his poetry. Tennyson wrote "Charge of the Light Brigade" and many others, but only the name made us think of the poet.

> *Half a league, half a league,*
> *Half a league onward,*
> *All in the valley of Death*
> *Rode the six hundred.*
> *"Forward, the Light Brigade!*
> *Charge for the guns!" he said:*
> *Into the valley of Death*
> *Rode the six hundred.*

Further on was the town of Fennimore—this is truly the literary section of the road. Although James Fenimore Cooper had only one "n," we gave the town literary license.

We returned to the Mississippi and Highway 35 (not the freeway) and enjoyed the view at Lynxville—an appropriate place for a Link to pause.

April 5
The Grand Round—Minneapolis, Minnesota

IN THE MORNING, Mike had a chance to ride a large portion of the Grand Round, reminding us, again, of what a great city for bikes this is. We were amazed by the numbers of people on the trails. It was a very windy day and they were out despite the conditions, enjoying the sunshine and the beauty of the Mississippi River, Minnehaha Creek, and the Chain of Lakes.

Beginning at the Stone Arch Bridge and St. Anthony Falls, Mike tried to go north along the river but found that the trail only went three miles so he crossed over by the old Hamm's beer plant. This old castle of a building is now offices and there is a wonderful new library on one end that was having a book sale. Nearby is the Arts District and Mike rode up to Glueck Park, but there were no more river trails, and the road was under construction so it was back to Boom Island, where the excursion boats dock.

The trail crosses over an iron bridge to Nicollet Island, where the path is nicely wooded until we came up to the railroad grade, De LaSalle High School, and the Nicollet Island Inn. We left the island by a second iron bridge—this one for cars as well as bikes and pedestrians. Along this route, a biker or hiker can move from the industrial northeast to the downtown cityscape.

There are wonderful views of the Stone Arch Bridge, which once was traversed by trains. It is a pedestrian biking trail now with excellent scenery up- and downriver. The Milling District, St. Anthony Falls, and the Gorge are all easy to see and photograph from the old railroad bridge. Downstream is the memorial to the victims of the I-35W bridge collapse. It is well done and emphasizes both our fragility and the randomness of events that determine our lives. The bridge collapsed suddenly August 1, 2007, killing thirteen people and injuring 145. Considering that it was rush hour, it was amazing there wasn't even more loss of life.

The river route is enjoyable for views of the university, the limestone bluffs, and the people enjoying the parks, ducks, geese, and sunshine. The trail dips to the river level at Riverside Park and then goes back up to the blufftop leading to the Ford Lock and Dam—Lock #1. From here, Mike chose to go along Minnehaha Creek rather than on to Fort Snelling. Both are good rides, but he was supposed to meet me for lunch and this meant creating a circle. It was no effort—Minnehaha Park is the state's oldest, originally designated as a state park, but never left the city's jurisdiction.

The creek is wooded, shady, protected from the wind and winds through south Minneapolis neighborhoods all the way to Lake Harriet and past Lake Nokomis.

By this time, Mike came to realize that his sixty-six-year-old body was not ready to compete with those who disregard the ten-mile-per-hour speed limit requested for the trail. He was passed by numerous bikers and only passed a few (they were stopped).

At the Chain of Lakes, bikers must ride in one direction, and where he joined the trail he turned the wrong way. There is a one-way marker. It was not an error that would last long and he traveled the right route around Lake Harriet, Calhoun, Lake of the Isles (some might remember this from the opening of the old *Mary Tyler Moore* television show) and up past Kenwood park and back down to the sculpture garden and over to Loring Park.

By this time Mike knew I could not make lunch time and had seen a small urban farmer's market beside the Guthrie, where he returned to have good food and wait. It was a wonderful ride—a forty-mile loop filled with photos, neat places, and good exercise.

Chapter Six

The Upper Mississippi Above Commericial Navigation

KATE

May 28, 2013
Itasca to Bemidji

THICK GRAY CLOUDS filled the sky on this late May day when we arrived at the parking lot in Itasca State Park. This is where history, according to Henry Schoolcraft, designates the origins of the great river of North America. Even though we were not following the river sequentially, we would get in a canoe and travel from this point downriver and add it to a year of experiences. Our plans had changed as an unusually long winter dragged into what we normally consider summer. The ice was still thick on the lakes in northern Minnesota until May 22, preventing us from our hoped-for March or April start.

Our friend and neighbor Dick Glattly was with us for this portion of the Mississippi adventure and we met another longtime friend, Jim Fitzpatrick, in the park. Jim had recently retired as the director of Carpenter Nature Center and was now able to pursue his many outdoor interests. Canoeing had been a lifelong passion and he had covered countless miles of the Boundary Waters Canoe Area as well as wilderness areas in Canada. He had an old Airstream trailer he used as a cabin not far away from Itasca, and he had offered it as an overnight accommodation for the three of us.

It was well past noon when we met Jim in the parking lot. After talking about the distance we hoped to cover that afternoon, we unloaded the two canoes and carried them to the put-in spot, just fifty feet below the famous string of rocks that cross the water as it empties from Lake Itasca into the little stream that is the Mississippi. As I approached the headwaters, I heard much laughing and squealing. A big group of middle school kids on an end-of-the-year field trip were splashing in the cold water. Their exuberance and excitement was in stark contrast to the trepidation

I was feeling about our soon-to-commence paddle. I had a lot of time to contemplate what might be ahead of us, while Mike and the other men drove the trucks to the point where we planned to end the day. This is known as "setting up the shuttle." My anxiety was based on the fact that we really didn't know what the water level was or the difficulty of maneuvering the small, rocky stream. What I had seen looked narrow and twisty, with overhanging tree branches. We would first pass under one very low bridge followed by another bridge, after which the stream turned and disappeared into the unknown.

When the guys returned we got into the canoes. It was now 3:30 P.M. Mike and I were in the first boat, Jim and Dick in the second. Mike and I have been canoeing partners for nearly thirty years and our movements are almost intuitive at this point, which makes our comfort and confidence in the canoe reassuring. Jim and Dick, having just met, had no such experience to base their decisions on, such as who would be in the stern and who would be in the bow, nor how they would communicate about how to negotiate the challenges ahead. Dick chose to take the stern and Jim accepted the bow spot. Both are big men with old knees that don't let them kneel down in front of the seats, a position that gets the paddler's center of gravity lower in the boat—useful for balancing. As we approached the first bridge, my apprehension grew. There were people on it watching our approach. They were probably as skeptical as I, or looking

forward to some entertainment at our expense. I didn't think we'd make it under, but Mike insisted we would and said, "Duck down." When we were almost touching the bridge I bent as low as possible and we made it through. Whew! Then we turned to watch the other canoe, holding our breath. But they made it, too.

The next bridge was higher, but had a fast current under it that took us down to the first hazard—a sweeper (tree branch hanging low over the water) on river left. Mike and I made the sharp right-hand turn and kept going until we heard a clunk and looked back to see Dick and Jim's canoe go over. The water was shallow, so they could stand up, but I immediately thought about the expensive camera Jim had around his neck. That, his expensive camera lens, and iPhone all got soaked. Mike and I waited along the edge of the stream while they emptied the water out of their canoe, got back in, and came on. The air temperature that day was in the fifties and since it was late in the afternoon, would not be getting any warmer. The stream soon deposited us in a thick, vast marsh.

Dick and Jim called out that they needed to stop. There was a crack in their canoe on the side next to the stern seat and water was coming in. Thank God for duct tape. The leak stopped and we moved onward once again. The marsh consisted of old brown cattail stalks, with just barely new green growth showing. The twists and turns began. This would become a familiar pattern for the next two days. Back and forth we went, through the maze of marsh. Very few birds were singing in this first portion of the marsh, but gradually we began to hear more. There was a great crested flycatcher, then a common yellowthroat, rose-breasted grosbeak, black-throated blue warbler, red-eyed vireo, and sedge wren. We didn't see these songbirds, but welcomed their songs. We did see mallards, Canada geese, and an eagle. A merlin swept past, cliff swallows burst out from under bridges, barn swallows, too, and many red-winged blackbirds, the males perched on the old cattails displaying their scarlet epaulets.

Low, bushy willows were just starting to leaf out. The water beneath our canoes was clear and moving relatively fast. White shells studded the sandy bottom. Suddenly the marsh ended, and we were back into trees and an area of rapids, which were basically random rocks just below the surface. The combination required real canoe skills to successfully negotiate. Dick had told Jim he was "comfortable in the stern," but he really wasn't prepared

for this type of canoeing. They fell behind us and we saw them flip again. We waited to see them start up, and then we took off in the fast-moving water. We could no longer look back to see how they were doing because the narrow, rocky stream required too much concentration. We were stopped by one tree that was down all the way across—no way to go over it except getting out into a thick, sucking muck. Mike and I were working at it when Jim and Dick appeared. They both looked exhausted by this point and then Jim stepped out of the canoe and went up past his knee in a hole.

We began again and they fell behind us. We worried about them as we came upon two trees that had fallen across the stream. I looked at them and yelled back to Mike that I didn't think we could make it through. He assured me we could. It took perfect aim on Mike's part and as we neared the narrow, tiny opening, Mike shouted to me to drop to the bottom of the canoe. In an awkward acrobatic move I slipped under the bow seat and held my breath as we just barely slid beneath the trunk. I don't know how Mike got low enough, but we made it through. Again, decades of experience in canoes allowed Mike to judge what could and could not be done. Jim told Mike later, "I couldn't figure out how you got through some of those places."

We came under one bridge and there was a sharp turn to the right. We didn't make it and ran our bow straight into a small tree. We remained upright and moved away from it, but when I told Dick about it later and asked if he remembered that spot, he said, "I can't remember, but we probably dumped there, too. I've kinda lost count." It had been a really rough day for him. I think he knew Jim was a better paddler and that they might not have had such trouble if he had taken the stern. He was already talking about Jim taking the stern the next day and maybe them "having better luck with a different captain in charge." It was close to 7:00 P.M. when we finally pulled out of the river where the truck was parked. Thank goodness for long daylight hours.

After the guys ran the shuttle, we loaded the canoes up and drove back to Jim's place on Lake Minerva. His great-grandfather bought the land for duck hunting back in 1905, and Jim uses the 1970s-era Airstream trailer for his cabin. It was definitely a bachelor-type of place. There was a small bedroom with two beds at one end and a futon-like couch at the other "living room" end with a small galley kitchen and tiny bathroom between the two. Jim had just reopened the "cabin" after a long winter break and the mice

had enjoyed his residence in his absence. It was on the second night that I noticed the mouse pellets on top of the dark blue sheets we'd been sleeping on.

Since it was so late when we got there and we were all exhausted, we decided to go out to eat. Jim took a shower, but the rest of us just went as is—though Dick changed into dry clothes and used a pair of bungee cords as suspenders since his belt was soaked. We ate at the Lobo Den, a local hangout where burgers were the main entrée and images of wolves were the main décor.

Back at the Airstream, the guys sipped scotch, and I sat on the couch wishing I had a spot where I could go to read, write, or whatever. I'm just not into guy BS. I started to fall asleep in my boredom, and it must have been about 10:30 when everyone decided to go to bed. Surprisingly, I wasn't awakened or kept awake by snoring, but by the regular opening and closing of the door and screen door which was right next to our "bed." Old men who drink lots in the evening spend half the night going out to pee.

May 29

THE NEXT MORNING DAWNED with a mix of sun and clouds. Dick was up by 7:00 A.M., but the morning moved slowly from there; lots of coffee to be made and drunk, especially by Jim. Then there was discussion of the day and the route and distance, lots of studying the map. We finally went back to the river via County Road 2, where we took out the day before. Going down the steep, grassy slope, Dick slipped and hurt his bad right knee. To add injury to insult, he was now limping badly.

While there, we heard and then saw black-billed magpies! Mike and I couldn't believe it. These are birds of the grassland and western mountain regions, but Jim told us he'd had them nest on his property. We saw them at the takeout on the next day, too. The guys left to drop off the vehicles, and I went up on the bridge to talk to a couple sitting on the railing and looking down at the river. They were from Georgia and had dropped off their twenty-two-year-old son and a buddy at the headwaters two hours earlier. I told them it took us four hours the day before, partly because of the difficult conditions. They claimed these guys, Robby and Linton, were capable Iraq vets who came up with the idea to paddle the length of the Mississippi while on their tour of duty. The couple wanted to wait until they came through to take some photos of them. I wished them luck (all of them). When the guys returned, we loaded into the canoes (Jim in the stern) and took off, waving to the Georgians on the bridge. It was 11:20 A.M.

Common yellowthroats and white-throated sparrows sang to us as we paddled onward. Other birds heard and seen included the American goldfinch, yellow warblers, song sparrows, alder flycatcher, pileated woodpecker, kingfisher, golden-winged warbler, and spotted sandpiper. Forster terns flew over us, cackling as they went. A bald eagle sat perched on a dead snag close to the water with his right wing drooping down. He looked as if he had just taken a dip in the water. He did not have a fully white head or tail. Jim, who has years of experience with captive birds of prey, said it was between four and five years old. Juneberries were in bloom, as were the pretty pink-flowered plums. Mammals on this day included a beaver that swam out and dived in front of us and a fat porcupine perched in the skinny branches of an aspen.

We paddled through marsh all day, it seemed. Coffee Pot Landing was our lunch stop. While there I got an excellent look (with binoculars) at a golden-winged warbler. I watched him sing in his glorious gold, black, and white splendor. There was a bridge at this spot, apparently for snowmobiles, and it led to a camping area on the other side, with the welcome amenity of an outhouse.

After Coffee Pot we got back into the trees and had some more challenges, including going through a couple downed trees where there was just a partial opening in the branches. Then we came to another obstruction—a large downed tree that we decided was best not gone over in the canoe. This was in the Stump Rapids section. We pulled to the left and decided we'd have to lift the canoe out of the water and over the trunk where it joined the bank. I got out first and ended up climbing onto the trunk to help maneuver the canoe. Dick and Jim were right behind us and after managing to get our boat back into the water, we got in and waited for them to do the same thing. Dick had to manage it with his gimpy leg. I was worried he'd have trouble getting back into his seat, but he and Jim both managed it, and we were underway again, back into more marsh. The day ended at 5:10 P.M., having covered 16.3 miles.

May 30

IT WAS CLOUDY and misting at 9:00 A.M. Mike, Dick, and I drove to the Itasca Park Visitor Center hoping to buy a rain poncho for Mike, but it wasn't open yet. Then the three of us—in two vehicles—started driving to the put-in where Jim would be waiting. Along the way we decided we should just drive to the take-out spot since we were already partway there, leave one vehicle and then go to the start. This was a good plan, although we didn't have a good map to help us take the shortest route, and we had no way of letting Jim know what we were doing. We finally got to the bridge where he was waiting and put into the river at 10:50 A.M.

It was still cloudy and now raining lightly. Jim and Dick started ahead of us. Swallows were swarming out from under the bridge when we set off. When we caught up with Jim and Dick, a small flock of six trumpeter swans flew overhead, honking the whole way. It was a glorious sight that was only captured by our memories, since I was unable to capture it with my camera. We were in thick marsh again. Jim had paddled this part of the river before, but for Mike, Dick, and I, this was one of the big revelations about the Mississippi River, that so much of its beginning is actually vast marshlands. It is reminiscent of the Everglades, where water flows not in a single channel, but spread out in a vast wetland complex. A flock of black terns swooped back and forth, calling above us. They are beautiful, graceful birds with sharp pointed wings, not commonly seen in other parts of the state, but this seems like a popular breeding area for them.

Rain began to fall in earnest, and we put on our gear and got wet. Jim and Mike had commented on the lack of rails (heard or seen) but no sooner had they said it than we heard a black rail, then a Virginia, and finally a sora. These birds of the wetlands are rarely seen as they are well camouflaged for the marshland habitat they prefer. Most people learn to identify them by their calls. A parula warbler sang from shoreline trees. This is the same species we heard in Louisiana in March. Some migrate to these far northern forests to nest, while others remain in the deep south and nest in the swamp forests. We saw few ducks, but a blue-winged teal startled us as it bolted skyward out of the vegetation.

We pulled off for lunch at a spot we thought was Bear Den Campground. It wasn't. It was a spot used by snowmobilers in the winter, evidenced by the long wooden dock that had been pulled up on shore. We

tied up there and all three creaky male bodies unfolded and stumbled to shore. I was the youngest member of the group, and luckily all my joints are still in good condition. Mike had extreme pain and trouble with his ankles. He got some ribbing from the other two since he had bragged earlier about his better physical condition. We looked for some logs to sit on, but ended up coming back to the wooden dock where we each sat and ate our lunch of venison sausage and leftover salmon from the last night's dinner (both thanks to Dick), fresh cherries, and a mix of snack crackers.

As he often does, Mike wandered off down a trail just as the sun started to break through the clouds. I stood on the dock looking at the river and heard voices. Suddenly a canoe came into view. It was the two young men from Georgia. When they got closer they said hi, and I asked how it went for them on that first stretch of the river. They said not too bad, though they did tip once. They had stayed at Coffee Pot the night before drying out their stuff. They told us there were some canoes behind them, and sure enough here came two more canoes—very lightweight, fast ones with a male and female couple in each. They hailed us and asked where we were headed. When I told them, "my husband and I are trying to do the entire river in a combination of different boats," one young man

at the back of one canoe said, "I saw you at Duluth Pack" (the Full Circle talk we gave the past winter). That was a fun connection. He was from French River, Minnesota. All four seemed very comfortable and skilled in their canoes, and they were headed all the way to the Gulf of Mexico, too.

They paddled on, we finished our lunch break, and Mike came back just after the others paddled away. We got back in our boats, shoved off, and passed the two guys eating their lunch while sitting in their canoe next to the bank. I told them we'd put them on our "Full Length Mississippi" Facebook page. Shortly thereafter, we passed Bear Den campsite where the other two canoes had stopped for their lunch break.

As we paddled past all the thick cattails a beaver surprised me by sliding into the water right next to our canoe. We probably gave him a shock, too. Jim and Dick saw it swim out behind us. This marsh was unlike any we had been in before. It opened up into a lake and we found the way out, but then it became more difficult. Jim seemed most able to read the current and pick the right branch to follow. The other clue was to look into the water (where we could) and see which way the vegetation lay. However, we also had a headwind the whole time so the surface water had waves coming toward us, making it extra hard to see the current. The channels swerved back and forth. We could easily see where we wanted to go, but we had to go far to our right and then left before we got there. Looking back, we could see the unattached heads of the two Georgians moving along the channels behind us.

Lots of cottony seeds from willows or aspens floated in the air. An osprey soared overhead, swamp sparrows sang, and we saw a great blue heron standing in the shallows. Some Canada geese flew over and so did a sandhill crane. It did rain a bit after lunch, but then with the wind picking up, the clouds broke up into all sorts of cumulus, many with dark, flat bottoms. Some bubbled up into towering, glowing mountains.

At this point the river was two canoe lengths wide. On the first day, it was barely one canoe length wide. There were supposed to be two tributaries entering the river on this stretch but we couldn't be sure where they were, since they had to go through marsh. The ubiquitous red-winged blackbirds let us know they did not like our intrusion and a long-billed marsh wren called from the dry stalks, too. We passed a tall, curved, sandy bank where there were holes suitable for the nests of the kingfisher that we saw fly out.

By the later afternoon, both Mike and I were losing steam, which did not make me any happier when Mike decided to go to the right instead of following Jim to the left. His hunch was wrong, and we ended up making a big, extra circle. My mood improved as we watched a pair of broad-winged hawks chase each other through the trees, and in the distance the aspens displayed that lovely spring green shade we wait nearly eleven months to see each year.

We ended our day just past the Old Iron Bridge campsite. While the guys ran the shuttle I waited with the canoes with the sun hot on my neck and back and wondered whether I'd see any of the other canoe groups. It wasn't until the guys returned that we saw the two canoes with the Minnesotans in them. We should have asked if they'd seen the Georgians. It would be so easy to take the wrong channel in that vast, mazelike marsh. A day later, we talked to a county sheriff about this stretch of the river and he said people have gotten lost. The previous year, one man had to spend the night in the marsh in his canoe because he got lost and hadn't brought any matches with him, let alone a flashlight.

Dick headed back home at the end of the day and Mike and I headed into Bemidji to spend the night at a hotel. Jim wasn't sure if he'd join us the next day on the river. It would depend on the weather conditions.

May 31

THE NEXT DAY, we found ourselves in a section of the river with lots of fallen trees. We had heard about this beforehand from a DNR representative. Crews had been out trying to clear them but it was slow work, especially with the cold spring we had been having. Interspersed with the trees were exposed rocks, so it really was a challenge course as we negotiated our way through. We were getting closer to Bemidji on this stretch, too, so we began to see more homes along the banks.

We ended our paddle on the county road just before Lake Irving. Earlier in the day we had left Mike's bike at a gift shop, so we pulled out in a small marshy bay below the property. We ate a quick lunch on the bank and then Mike retrieved his bike and began riding back to the car. I went up to the red barn and the owner of the shop let me in to wait.

June 1

We bypassed the wind-turbulent lakes and joined our old friend, Tim Whitfeld, to canoe to Grand Rapids. Tim, from England, had a mixed career in the natural sciences, working at the Audubon Center with us and at Princeton, where he worked in their herbarium—hardly comparable jobs. Then

he completed his doctorate at the University of Minnesota with research in New Guinea, followed by work at the university, and would begin a job at the Brown University herbarium after paddling with us.

It was hardly New Guinea weather—the wind was still blowing across Lake Winnibigoshish and mixed with rain when we put in below the dam. This was one of forty-three dams that would challenge us as we made our way towards St. Louis, Missouri. Our route was on a much wider river now, and we moved downstream sharing stories as Tim paddled a solo boat. In Little Winni, the winds caught us again and we could not be near each other since the waves were building on the south end, where we had to exit. It was the biggest excitement of the day.

Lunch at a campsite gave us time to catch up with each other, check out the plants, and get some needed energy. Downstream, the river wound in and out of muddy flats and lots of low wetland vegetation. We had to deal with lots of wind and occasional rain as we dropped below Highway 2 and down to a park where we had left our car for this shuttle.

We got the cars and went to Schoolcraft State Park, where we would camp for the night. It is a small park along the Mississippi with a mix of shoreline features. According to historical records, Schoolcraft actually

camped here on his Mississippi source expedition, so it was an appropriate place for us. Food, talk, a little scotch, and a good night sleep made us ready for the next day.

We entered the river where we had taken out—across from the Leech River that comes out of Leech Lake. Zebulon Pike had turned here and claimed Leech Lake for the headwaters in 1806, when he did a north/south expedition that rivaled the Lewis and Clark Expedition of a year earlier.

The river was pleasant and the sun was out. We could see wood ducks and loons cruise down well-defined channels and only occasionally had to fight a sideways gust of wind. We saw water lilies rising from the bottom of the river—not in flower, but rather large leaf systems floating to the surface. There were some dragonflies and a sense that we had entered into a different river. The riverbanks were further from the river than upstream. It was not marshland, but muddy banks lined with grasses and sedges, and the forests were further from us. Eagles still flew from the trees, but already we had a sense of a different type of river.

The Lakes

MIKE

ONE OF THE THINGS I did not anticipate when the ice and snow prevented us from an April and early May paddle was the fact that when I had the opportunity to get back to boating between guiding obligations, it would allow me to see the river in many seasons and variations. The river flows north from Lake Itasca and enters Irving and a sequence of lakes, reaching its furthest north on the outlet from Lake Bemidji, from where it travels eastwardly through Lake Winnibigoshish and then begins seeking its southern route through Little Winni.

We were blocked by winds when we paddled the upper portion and returned the first week of August to see this section of moraine-clustered lake with Kate's mom. She was celebrating her ninetieth year and joined us for a portion of the river and to catch a fish. Instead of the brown marsh grasses and cattails from our first trip through this region we were seeing them in full green—towers of plants, thick mats of vegetation. The birds were not hunting for nests, but rather training their young.

The Mississippi enters Lake Irving through a shallow marsh and exits into Lake Bemidji under four bridges—bike, railroad, and old and new road bridges. As we exited the lake there was a series of red and green buoys to mark the route for power boats, and each of the floats had a young black tern sitting on top. The adults were flying around and periodically diving down to feed the begging young. We had never seen young black terns, which are white with black smudges on their face. A Forster's tern took the outermost buoy and seemed agitated by the begging young. (This might be our imagination—but we did see him have a conflict with another tern that wanted his post.)

Lake Bemidji is a long lake oriented north/south and the wind was blowing from the north on our trip across the lake, making the water dark and rough. The Mississippi exits on the northeast side of the lake, making the direct route a diagonal path. We enjoyed seeing Paul Bunyan and Babe the Blue Ox from the water before crossing. These statues are landmarks of Bemidji, which we had never seen from the water. Legend has it this lake is Paul's footprint, and it does have the right shape.

Several loons entertained us as we crossed the open water. We negotiated a large mat of bulrush that dominated the lake near the river exit. Here we found loons, pelicans, gulls, and ducks all avoiding the open-water waves. The Ojibwe called this lake Bemijigamaag-zaaga'igan, which translates roughly to "traversing lake," which describes its part on the route of the Mississippi.

The river here is raised and calmed by the Ottertail Dam, the first of many dams we would see on our way to the Twin Cities. Homes lined the areas where the banks were high and the river narrow. Wild rice and other aquatic plants filled the wide spots. Once again we were entertained by loons, but here they were young, fuzzy, brown young swimming beside their parents. A few ducks were among the vegetation and as we approached the dam the water grew shallow as it widened. In this area, we found thick bassweed, one of many Potamogeton species of aquatic submerged plants that fill the waters.

At Wolf Lake the river enters from the north and slips out the northeast corner. The lake continues south. Once again, the river serves more as a boat channel or marina than a moving body, with lots of houses but also some extensive marsh. We found a family of goldeneyes as well as mallards and wood ducks along this section. Next, the river enters Lake Andrusia from the west and exits on the southern end. It is another long north/south lake. Each of the last three lakes stretch out in the direction of glacial movement and probably reflect stream flow during the glacial melt stages.

Cass Lake, however, the next on our journey, probably has its origin from buried ice blocks that melted and left big kettles to fill with water. I like the original lake name: Gaa-miskwaawaawaakokaag, which means "where there are many red cedar." The French translated the name to Lac du Cedre Rouge and the English called it Red Cedar Lake. Now it is named for General Lewis Cass, who led an 1820 expedition to find the source of the Mississippi. He found it difficult to navigate beyond this lake so he declared it the source of the river. Henry Schoolcraft was with Cass and would come back later to designate Itasca as the true source (makes one wonder if he wasn't happy with the declaration by Cass and the opportunity to return later).

We entered Allen Bay on the west end and proceeded to cross the seven miles of lake to the eastern outflow at Knudson Dam. Along the route we passed Star Island, a very large land mass with its own lake—Windigo. Cass is the eleventh largest lake in Minnesota and eighth largest within the state borders, excluding Lake Superior, Lake of the Woods, and Rainy Lake.

After passing the island we entered the large central bowl of the lake, which can become really wavy, and we were happy to pass without the winds agitating the waters earlier in the spring. Knudson Dam is a small dam that serves to hold the water level within the lake. Originally the lake was larger, with a shallow area connecting it to Pike Bay in the south, but railroad and road construction severed the natural connection, which has now been replaced by a channel that still lets boaters travel between them.

Knutson Dam was originally a logging dam and is now maintained by the Forest Service, which controls a large area surrounding these lakes—the Chippewa National Forest. The Leech Lake Band of Ojibwe has an office and a large presence in the Cass Lake area.

Between Cass Lake and Lake Winnibigoshish the vegetative mats had given way and floated out into the original channel, making the water filter through large curtains of cattails. We tried twice to find routes through and failed. With the summer vegetation at its peak, boaters will have a real challenge going downstream.

We went upstream from Winnibigoshish and enjoyed the fact that this portion of the river is wild and filled with water lilies—both yellow and white—a beaver lodge, gulls, eagles, white pelicans, and ducks. Big Winni is the largest challenge on the upper river and technically the widest place on the Mississippi (eleven miles for trivia buffs). Crossing is from the west side to the eastern bay, where the dam is located.

The name comes from the Ojibwe Wiinibiigoonzhish, which means filthy or brackish water—probably because it was so wide and shallow, making the waters opaque with suspended matter. The root name is probably responsible for Lake Winnipeg's name in Canada, too. Lake Winnibigoshish is the fourth-largest lake within Minnesota, behind Red Lake, Mille Lacs, and Leech and ahead of Vermilion, Kabetogama, Mud (Marshall County), Cass, and Minnetonka. Winni is 58,544 acres and seventy

feet deep at the maximum. A good lake map shows the old river valley in the bottom contours. Before the dam, it would have been an area of extensive aquatic vegetation, wild rice, ducks, fish, and furbearers. The lake accounts for fourteen miles of Mississippi River, but paddlers can seldom go in a straight line because of winds and waves.

Grand Rapids to Sartell

THE EVOLUTION OF A RIVER is a gradual process of accretion—the addition of small streams, rivers, and springs. The movement of water from one geographic area to another creates a valley that deepens as it flows to the ultimate low point: the ocean. Rivers increases in strength with the addition of each neighboring waterway. This is the strength of the watershed, and it became increasingly apparent as we moved downstream from the narrow source. By the time we reached Highway 6 just west of Grand Rapids, Minnesota, the river had increased significantly and it was time to move to the second of our boats.

A river system changes its biological dynamics as it grows. In the initial stages the river is fed by the leaves and debris that grow along the shore. This organic matter joins snowmelt, springs, and rain to create the initial biological system. In the water are shredders like stoneflies (if the water is of good quality), crane flies, and caddis fly nymphs. Shredders take apart the organic matter that falls in the water and prepare another level of nutrients in the water. Upstream in the clear, cold water are mayfly nymphs that require nonpolluted water, as do the stoneflies and blackfly larva. The blackfly is one of our least favorite organisms, along with deer flies, horse flies, ticks, and mosquitoes, but they do indicate good water quality and highly oxygenated places such as rapids and falls. Their predators are fish—walleye in murky, wave-agitated waters and bass, northerns, and dobsonfly larva elsewhere.

At this stage, we were in the middle river as far as biology was concerned. Here are the midge and mayfly "collectors" and crane fly larva shredders. Dragonfly larva and beetle larva are the predators, along with the fish, and mayflies, snails, limpets, and caddis fly larva are the grazers.

This part of the adventure would be a real treat because my neighbor, Dick Glattly, and I had rescued a twelve-foot Montgomery Ward fishing boat, replaced the transom, the seats, and the floatation and rebuilt a

1974 Johnson fifteen-horsepower motor that had been left in a shed at the Audubon Center for a number of years. Sitting on the dirt floor, untouched by humans, it became a residence for rodents who found a way in that we could not explain. Removing the cover of the motor we found a solid wall of insulation and acorns packed into the carburetor, the air intake, and every other inch of open space. The nest in all likelihood had been enjoyed by more than one generation. The wires had served as chew toys and had to be spliced and replaced, but overall the Johnson held up well and with a minimum of effort we brought it back to life.

The little boat and motor rode on a trailer that had been restored, too. I put in with the help of Dick at the same point that the canoe left the river. This was a new experience, since I had previously paddled the river all the way to La Crosse. The little boat, with me as its lone passenger, moved smoothly through the twisting channels. Downstream at Grand Rapids were two dams, and they created two reservoirs that effectively removed the current. From the Highway 6 bridge the channels continued to widen and slow, but the marsh was healthy with birds and two loons that let the boat ease up beside them while they swam, dove, and showed no distress.

Three paddlers in kayaks were easing their way south. They were from New Orleans and were going home. It was a cool idea.

Turning one corner changed the entire sense of the river. Sprawled across the horizon was a power plant. It was like an encounter with an extra-terrestrial. Suddenly the marsh that had expanded into a broad and shallow lake was invaded by boxy buildings and smoking towers.

The little fifteen-horse struggled through the vegetation. It was thick to the surface. No channels were present, only flocks of goldeneye ducks. As the lake began to narrow, three options presented themselves. Thanks to the GPS unit, I chose the right one—the one that looked least likely. Downstream an otter surfaced and dove in another thick area of vegetation as ring-billed gulls flew across.

After navigating a river-like channel, the dam was ahead and Dick was at the landing to help move the boat past this dangerous obstruction. This is an Army Corp of Engineers park with camping, picnic, boat ramp, and fishing. Lots of people were enjoying the fast water shooting below the dam, trying for fish or just relaxing. A large group of Canada geese herded their young—a day camp for goslings—and one of the adults hissed as I took photos. Near a picnic table a group of law enforcement personnel were practicing some form of restraint techniques and downstream were many campers.

We put in again on the Blandin pond. This time Dick joined me and we motored up to the Corp's dam and then back downstream to the Company dam. This was a pretty lake with a white pine island and both loons and mallards for entertainment. After the eight-mile round trip it was to the Dairy Queen for refreshments. Looking at the two dams and thinking about the city name, I could only wish I could have seen the five-foot drop over a third of mile that gave the location its name. This is the home of the Blandin paper mill and the ride over the lake gave us a view of the extensive piles of logs and the massive operation that has supported the local economy since 1891.

Below the dam was a classical Midwestern river system—banks of silver maples and ash, a few homes, an occasional bridge and lots of quiet beauty. Green walls were broken up by large sand banks that dropped precipitously into the stream. Small herds of cattle were startled by my sudden appearance. Near the La Prairie River, I met a professional fisherman from Minneapolis who was heading to the Gulf of Mexico.

The trip had eight eagles to entertain me on the way to Jacobsen, along with numerous spotted sandpipers and kingfishers, each leapfrogging around the next bend and then waiting to be upset and move on again at the next corner.

Dick joined me at one put-in clad in a bug suit that made him look like an alien. It was the beer in his hand that caused me to stop. He jumped in, and we enjoyed the beverage on the river—on shore the mosquitoes had hatched; it was no place to sit and relax.

From Jacobsen to Palisades, Dick rode with me. The challenge around the bends was to avoid the trees that had fallen in—sometimes both on the inside and outside of curves. Seven more bald eagles were on this stretch and the water increased in width from the Sandy Lake inlet and the Swan River.

Lots of great-crested flycatchers, vireos, and scarlet tanagers were in the trees and the shoreline had a wonderful wilderness feeling with very few houses. It was along this stretch we met a man, we think in his early sixties, and his mother(!) canoeing to the Gulf. They were from Georgia, and they asked us to take their photos and email them to his wife, which I did. This unlikely duo had previously canoed an Arctic River together. I connected with the man's wife and was able to follow the journey as they successfully navigated to the Gulf of Mexico.

The best wildlife sighting was a hooded merganser with three chicks. The chicks scrambled into the shoreline vegetation, and the adult, a female, went to an urgent broken-wing act. She thrashed the water in apparent agony, but when she got too far from us she flew back and—obviously—suffered another broken wing.

Palisade does not seem to live up to the picture the name elicits, but according to the Minnesota Historical Society, the name was given by an official of the Soo Line for the high embankment on the Mississippi River.

Trying to get from Palisade downriver began with a flat tire on the trailer, but luckily Palisade has a wonderful gas station that does a good business in tires. It is a working station that actually fixes cars like they did when we were young. This was a lucky break, as I had already had trouble with the fuel line.

The scenery going downriver is a nice wooded landscape that gives a sense of peace and quiet. Since I was alone in the boat, it was a very reflective time, which was given a boost by wood ducks, mallards, and hooded mergansers doing their wing-flapping best to distract me from their young broods. A lone osprey sat in its nest on top of a power pole.

The most enjoyable aspect of this day was the flight of spotted sandpipers. There were now large families with new broods taking wing. Spooked by the boat's approach, they were like dolphins at sea, riding the air in front of the bow wave. Up to eight sandpipers would lift off and fly ahead of the boat, unintentionally guiding me downstream.

The woods of July were deep green and the songs were muted. The floating families provided the most entertainment, but kingfishers and kingbirds added to my observations.

Kate joined me the next day and we explored the waters above the Brainerd dam. In addition to the reservoir, a wide flat area was filled with vegetation and provided a difficult passage. We could not run the little fifteen-horse in one thick area and tried our best to paddle out with the oars. First we rowed, but the vegetation was so thick it made each oar impossibly heavy and the vegetation would not come off unless the oars were taken out of the locks and held vertically. This was not to Kate's pleasure, but it did allow us to observe numerous dragonflies that were both emerging and mating. A great blue heron flew in, landed, and watched us struggle inch by inch through the morass.

In this area of shallows we found a raft of feeding gulls, but what was really fun was the large number of black terns that were feeding and probably nesting in the shallows. At the south end of the natural lake they were lined up along the branches of an old tree. It was like a two-tiered bleacher and they sat and watched us just as we had watched them. In flight they hover and glide, picking off food from the surface, not plunging in the water like the Forster or common tern. Their head and bodies are dark black, but in flight you see white at the posterior end of the birds

and white "headlights" that decorate the leading edge of the wings. When sitting, they look darker.

Continuing downstream, we found another deer near the water's edge. It was obvious the deer was not there for water. It was instead standing in the water and eating the vegetation, its tail flicking away flies. Deer flies and horse flies are a terrible plague and this poor creature knew that open water, along with sun and wind, would help drive away the pests.

We went to the dam but pulled out in Rice Lake, another natural widening of the river. A mallard family scooted away from us and homes lined the shores as we found the park.

Below Brainerd Dam, the river level is much lower with small riffles. It passes the largest tributary in the area, the Crow Wing River, at Crow Wing State Park. This river park was the site of two missions, Catholic and Lutheran, that were set up to convert the Native Americans and the small community of Crow Wing. The community served the river traffic and was near the famous "Woods" ox cart trail that pioneers used to access the northwest prairies of Minnesota. The ox cart was the covered wagon of Minnesota—and a lot more work as people walked beside the cart and their laboring ox. Chippewa Overlook gives a good view of the river, which at this stage has large mud flats on both sides—and you do not want to step into the mud.

The Minnesota DNR website has the following description of the Crow Wing name:

> There is some disagreement about the origin of the name Crow Wing. Most agree that the nineteenth-century town, the county, and the state park honored the name of the river. Some claim that the river was so named because an island, prominently located at the confluence of the Mississippi and Crow Wing rivers, is shaped like a crow's wing. Others claim that the name is a mistranslation of an Ojibwe word for raven or raven feather. Still others say that the name is derived from the Little Crow chiefdom and lineage of the Dakota, who inhabited this region before the Ojibwe. According to historian William Warren, this was the scene of a major battle between the Dakota and Ojibwe Indians in 1768.

Below the state park is the National Guard's Fort Ripley, which was established in 1856. This large holding (53,000 acres) preserves a wonderful stretch of rivershore. The camp combines military preparedness and environmental concerns. Its webpage describes:

> Camp Ripley abounds with plant and animal life unique to central Minnesota. Surveys have identified 565 types of plants, 202 bird species, 41 species of fish, 107 types of aquatic invertebrates, 65 species of butterflies, 51 mammal species, 23 reptiles and amphibians, and 8 mussel species. Wildlife species of particular interest include the bald eagle, white-tailed deer, black bear, gray wolf and Blanding's turtle. With a population of 20-25 deer per square mile and its potential for trophy deer, Camp Ripley has been nationally recognized as having an exceptionally healthy deer herd. The Department of Natural Resources began monitoring the deer population at Camp Ripley in 1954, the first year of the annual white-tail bow hunt. Several Camp Ripley hunting opportunities are offered annually, including the Disabled American Veterans deer hunt (established in 1992).

Numerous logs had floated down the river and lodged in the waters above Little Falls. Most of these were above the water and could be avoided. Small branches called dead heads just peeked above the water and could hide when the water was disturbed, making it difficult to find and avoid these. I tried to be alert. However, there was a log lodged beneath the water with no ends showing, a water-logged trunk that just lurked there.

I passed over without knowing it was there until the little motor slid against and up and over the log. This action of sliding over raised the motor up and off the transom. It was quickly lifted, and then it was swimming and not happy. I was able to bring it back in after a struggle. A motor like this is a heavy dead lift when one is reaching over the transom and trying to wrestle it from the water. Luckily, when I lifted the cowling, I found no water inside. So I tried to start it. It nearly started, but at that point the starter cord snapped and there was nothing left to reattach. This left the oars.

It was not a bad row, except that a strong wind gusting to twenty-five miles per hour was blowing up the river. After four miles, a young man in a fishing boat came out of the backwaters and asked if I wanted a tow. I didn't hesitate, saying, "Yes, please." The cowling on his motor was off ,which seemed strange. He said last week he had problems and had to be towed in. He was "paying it forward"—a really nice gesture to follow.

At the boat dock, two men were putting in a pontoon and grabbed the boat line. The cowling on their boat was off, too. They had a problem they hoped they had fixed and were testing the engine. I brought the boat trailer down and then hit the algae on the ramp and went down—the younger man said, "I hope the rest of your day goes better. You should just go home and sit the rest of the day." I laughed—no banana peel was any slicker than algae. Luckily, the man had a cousin in Little Falls who fixed both cars and boat motors. I drove to Luberts, and he was willing to take the motor in and work on it the next morning.

Thankfully, the little motor survived and Luberts did a wonderful fast job. Kate had come to join me for the day, and we put in below the dam and explored the river to the Blanchard Dam. Along this skinny reservoir was the home of Charles Lindbergh, father of the famed aviator. Charles Lindbergh was famous well before his son took to the air because of his leadership in progressive politics. The younger Charles spent his youth here along the banks of the Mississippi and probably developed a lot of his environmental ethics while living here.

Below the Lindberg home is Pike Creek, named for Zebulon Pike, just as the reservoir at Little Falls is named Zebulon Pike Lake. This was the wintering spot for the expedition he was leading from New Orleans.

At the bottom of the reservoir rose the hydro-electric Blanchard Dam, the tallest dam on the Mississippi at forty-seven feet. Below it, the river became very shallow—not unusual for the summer months, and it was now the second week of August. The little motor could not float over the rocky rapids, so I did a lot of rowing on this section. Large sets of islands created numerous channels that were rocky or simply impassible. It was beautiful and a fun challenge to negotiate. Past the bridge from Rice, the water levels were more dependable. I saw geese in the water, and a pair of river otters scooted on to the east bank.

Coming around a large peninsula that Doug Wood, the writer/musician describes as "a little Florida," I watched for the telltale sign of his wife, Kathy's, beautiful garden. Kate and Doug were at his small dock. Across the river is Peace Rock. Benton County, one of the state's original nine counties established by the territorial legislature in 1849, describes Peace Rock as such ". . . A large granite outcropping along the Mississippi River in Watab Township. It was named Peace Rock in 1832 by Henry Schoolcraft when he charted the Mississippi. It was so named because it marked the 1825 boundary between the Chippewa territory to the north and the Sioux lands to the south." In 1836, the mapping expedition of Joseph Nicollet passed this rock and Nicollet commented, "It is the first rock above St Anthony Falls rising high above the river, making it all the more pleasing to behold."

The peninsula where Doug and Kathy have their historic log home was named Pine Point. The *St. Cloud Times* wrote, "It would be a sad mistake to have this last stand of white pine in Central Minnesota fall a victim of the lumberman's ax. If this is cut off it will take many years to produce an equally beautiful stand of white pine—and the beauty of Pine Point, only ten miles north of this city, is equally as grand and beautiful as that in Itasca Park that people travel hundreds of miles to see."

A lot of forces work against the preservation of natural places and loggers came in and removed the forest despite the prohibitions. On Doug's property, the twelve-inch white pines that were left have grown into a majestic grove that have now been protected with the land trust. These pines are the most beautiful place on the reservoir behind the Sartell Dam.

I landed the boat and returned to join Kate, Doug, and Kathy for a wonderful cook-out that was second only to the conversation shared around the table. The river is lucky to have people like the Woods who care about the land and the future.

Chapter Seven

Mississippi River National Park & Upper Mississippi Wildlife Refuge

MIKE

The Twin Cities

THE METRO RIVER really begins where the Rum River enters the Mississippi and joins the growing river volume. I will always have fond memories of this river because it is the place where I made my connection to nature. When I was twenty-one and recently moved to Champlin, I went through the apartment building introducing myself to the other residents. Neal Hayford was a plumber living down the hall and in our discussion he mentioned that his brother had a canoe we could borrow. The result was two novices floating down the Rum, not a wilderness river, but much more wild and undeveloped in the mid-sixties. What fascinated me was the constant change that each bend in the river created. Plants, homes, animals—it was all new and fascinating. I wanted more and this led to a lifetime of exploring waterways and even my first canoe trip down the Mississippi River—a fifty-mile float that ended at 3:00 A.M. with Neal's wife asking people to drive the river road to look for us.

The Coon Rapids Dam is an Anoka County Park and a Three Rivers Regional Park with picnic facilities, bike trails and access to the dam—in most years. Besides the dam, the park includes the river just downstream, past numerous small islands and fishing holes.

Below the dam are the Islands of Peace, which are part of the Anoka County Park and the Mississippi River National Recreation Area, administered by the National Park Service. The park is a quiet presence that incorporates existing city, county, and state facilities and unites the river system that passes through the Twin Cities. Many people enjoy it without realizing they are in a National Park system. The visitor center is equally obscure as a nook within the Science Museum of Minnesota.

But do not discount the importance of this umbrella park, as it helps us celebrate the seventy-two miles of the river that established the location of the Twin Cities. By my count, there are at least sixty-four units of interest that fall within the park and many of them are important to our experiences. I was able to take my three grandsons, Aren and Ryan Carlson and Matthew Lyon, with me on the Minneapolis portion of the river.

In past years I had led my graduate students on an all-day canoe trip through this region, from Coon Rapids Dam to Fort Snelling. It is a classic ride that can be arranged through Wilderness Inquiry if you do not have your own conveyance.

With my grandsons, we rode in my little boat from the lock at St Anthony Falls. The boys were fascinated by the barges being loaded with scrap metal, fertilizer, coal, twine, and asphalt. The lock was closed to recreational traffic and has since been closed to commercial, as well, since this is a possible access point for Asian carp. We can only hope it is not too late. Each lock they bypass allows the spread up more and more tributaries and, therefore, into more and more of our lakes.

On previous canoe trips through the cities with teachers and college students, I passed through this lock many times and I do regret that others

will not experience the deepest lock on the river. In 2011, 135 barges went through the locks. It only takes one opening for the carp to move into the upper river and from there through the tributaries to the fishing paradise of northern Minnesota.

The grandsons got to see the largest waterfall on the Mississippi, but today, while it is still impressive, it is but a shadow of itself as it roils down a metal apron that was put in to stabilize the drop. The original falls was undercut when overly ambitious business interests tried to tunnel through the falls and increase the power already fueling the logging and milling enterprises that first made St. Anthony. Now a proposal for a new regional park here might open up one side to expose the real drop.

In *Life on the Mississippi*, Mark Twain wrote of this area,

> Minneapolis is situated at the falls of St. Anthony, which stretch across the river, fifteen hundred feet, and have a fall of eighty-two feet—a waterpower which, by art, has been made of inestimable value, business-wise, though somewhat to the damage of the Falls as a spectacle, or as a background against which to get your photograph taken.
>
> Thirty flouring-mills turn out two million barrels of the very choicest of flour every year; twenty sawmills produce two hundred million feet of lumber annually; then there are woolen mills, cotton mills,

paper and oil mills; and sash, nail, furniture, barrel, and other factories, without number, so to speak. The great flouring-mills here and
at St. Paul use the "new process" and mash the wheat by rolling, instead of grinding it."

Below the falls, the river is calm and passes by the University of Minnesota and the rowing club. It is a popular recreational area with steep limestone and sandstone cliffs forming the walls of the canyon and parks filled
with trails for biking, hiking, and relaxing on both sides of the river. Paddling
down the gorge, you can see limestone blocks consisting of thin layers lying
askew—geologists call them books, and like all books, they have a tale to tell.

Below the Ford Dam, we rode on the *Jonathon Paddleford* excursion
boat. We took the boys on the old boat after exploring the Harriet Island
Park across from downtown St. Paul. This was the most important upriver
steamboat port. Minneapolis waters were working waters with too much
turbulence and energy. Even today's modern paddlewheels leave from St.
Paul and go downstream.

In this section of the river, Zebulon Pike reenters the story.

The Minnesota Historical Society describes the treaty signing for the
ceding of the land that would become the two cities like this:

In 1805 the Dakota ceded 100,000 acres of land at the intersection of the Mississippi and Minnesota rivers. Lieutenant Zebulon Pike negotiated the agreement so that the U.S. government could build a military fort there. Of the seven Indian leaders present at the negotiations, only two signed the treaty.

Pike valued the land at $200,000, but no specific dollar amount was written in the treaty. At the signing, he gave the Indian leaders gifts whose total value was $200. The U.S. Senate approved the treaty, agreeing to pay only $2,000 for the land.

Generally, the Indians who signed treaties did not read English. They had to rely on interpreters who were paid by the U.S. government. It is uncertain whether they were aware of the exact terms of the treaties they signed.

Minneapolis and St. Paul are located on the land that was ceded in 1805.

The military fort built at the confluence of the rivers, Fort Snelling, was not a fort that engaged in battle, but it did have many dignitaries like the artist and writer George Catlin visit. It became more of a tourist mecca than a military outpost and this served the area well. Artists painted Minnehaha Falls and inspired others such as Longfellow, who never did visit.

St. Paul to Hastings

WHILE THE GORGE straddles the two cities and provides a deep cut that removes the boater from the urban lifestyle, the downtown St Paul area is a stark contrast. Here the river is girdled and controlled between the city on one side and Harriet Island on the other. The towering city buildings peek out between and around natural areas until the river squeezes under the city's bridges, slides past numerous barges, encounters a slice of the river bluff again where the ancient St. Croix is now a railroad yard, and then turns south past the largest area of barge loading. It is impressive for its starkness.

While Catlin wrote about St. Paul being the new "fashionable tour" for Eastern travelers, Mark Twain came at the wrong time, as he explains in *Life On the Mississippi*.

> The season being far advanced when we were in New Orleans, the roses and magnolia blossoms were falling; but here in St. Paul it was the snow. In New Orleans we had caught an occasional withering breath from over a crater, apparently; here in St. Paul we caught a frequent benumbing one from over a glacier, apparently.

But I wander from my theme. St. Paul is a wonderful town. It is put together in solid blocks of honest brick and stone, and has the air of intending to stay. Its post-office was established thirty-six years ago; and by and by, when the postmaster received a letter, he carried it to Washington, on horseback, to inquire what was to be done with it. Such is the legend.

Twain reflects on the original settler of St. Paul, Pig's Eye Parrant, who sold liquor to the soldiers, Native Americans, and anyone else who stumbled by. It was kept in one of the caves, and the original name for the new settlement was Pig's Eye. Mark Twain, of course, liked that story and shares this perspective in his description of the area. It is a description that is apt all over the river.

> How solemn and beautiful is the thought, that the earliest pioneer of civilization, the van-leader of civilization, is never the steamboat, never the railroad, never the newspaper, never the Sabbath-school, never the missionary—but always whiskey! Such is the case. Look history over; you will see. The missionary comes after the whiskey—I mean he arrives after the whiskey has arrived; next comes the poor immigrant, with ax and hoe and rifle; next, the trader; next, the miscellaneous rush; next, the gambler, the desperado, the highwayman, and all their kindred in sin of both sexes; and next, the smart chap who has bought up an old grant that covers all the land; this brings the lawyer tribe; the vigilance committee brings the undertaker. All these interests bring the newspaper; the newspaper starts up politics and a railroad; all hands turn to and build a church and a jail—and behold, civilization is established for ever in the land. But whiskey, you see, was the van-leader in this beneficent work. It always is. It was like a foreigner—and excusable in a foreigner—to be ignorant of this great truth, and wander off into astronomy to borrow a symbol. But if he had been conversant with the facts, he would have said—Westward the Jug of Empire takes its way.

Passing barges and towboats, I found that the river becomes less congested with industry as I approached the Interstate 494 bridge. In this area I was disconcerted by the sludge in the water—it looked toxic. I would not want to touch it and certainly not swim in it. I wondered if it was even safe to breathe in the toxic fumes of the area.

I went past more convoluted chemical and petroleum facilities and yet there were large areas of trees and islands that were still gorgeous.

Near Stump Lake, the waters spread out. This is a natural wide area, but one drowned by the lock and dam that leads in to Hastings. The shallow wetland islands were beautiful in a sad way, covered with the blooms of the invasive purple loosestrife. Great egrets hunted the shallows, gulls sat on logs with white pelicans, and a few bald eagles and osprey flew over the wetlands. A towboat came downstream, a train roared by on the eastern side, and it became a perfect place to think about how the river had changed and the constant tension between nature and industry on this world-class waterway.

Hastings to Lake Pepin

"How about lunch in Red Wing?" Thus was born the boat ride with Bill Bixby on his eighteen-foot Lund Alaskan boat in June. Hastings is a wonderful little river community with a main street reminiscent of the larger Red Wing with brick façades. First established as a camp by soldiers from Fort Snelling to guard a blocked shipment, it soon became a trading post and was incorporated in 1857 with the middle name of future general and governor Henry Hastings Sibley. The name had been drawn from a hat. Until 1951, it was famous for the 1895 spiral horse bridge that crossed the river, and in 2013 it was getting a third bridge, opening up the road to the ever-increasing traffic demands. The river port grew because of the Vermilion River that enters near the St. Croix. The falls on the Vermilion provided waterpower that ran the gristmills. Today in a nearby park one can even find the remains of a mill operated by Alexander Ramsey. This famous Minnesotan has the county that holds St. Paul named after him. The National Park refers to the islands and byways that are across from Prescott, Wisconsin, as the Vermilion River Bottoms—a wonderfully pristine river, island, and backwater network.

It isn't far from Hastings to Prescott, Wisconsin, where the St. Croix enters the Mississippi. This mighty river, a National Wild and Scenic River, is second only to the Minnesota as a tributary along the Minnesota section of the river. Its waters are blue and clear in contrast with the muddy Mississippi and they seem to resist mixing, running side-by-side downriver below the town. This lack of mixing is seen in many of the rivers downstream.

In *Crossing Design Boundaries, Volume 1*, engineers and scientists try to determine the mechanics of mixing and separation. Both rivers have their own flow rate and they also have different temperatures, density, and suspended loads. These factors create a shear zone when they first meet

and depend on turbulence in the river course to help with the blending and mixing. Just like in the air, colder masses sink and warmer will flow over, meaning that the mixing may take even longer than the coloration separation that can be seen on the surface. In a 1948 study of the Missouri and Mississippi rivers, the results found, "At St. Louis, the flows of the Missouri and upper Mississippi rivers are not homogeneously mixed, and, because the Missouri River usually has a higher concentration of suspended sediment than does the upper Mississippi, each flow can generally be identified by the appearance of the water." ("Fluvial Sediment of the Mississippi River at St. Louis, Missouri," by Paul Jordan. *Geological Survey Water-Supply Paper 1802*.)

Prescott's marina's is at the confluence and has a history that dates back to 1839, when Philander Prescott opened a trading post.

From the water, the twin-domed towers on the 1912 St Joseph Catholic Church and the "mouse ears" look of the weights on the vertical lift bridge over the St. Croix are the most prominent landmarks. The number of fishermen out in boats indicates this is a good place for catching fish. It made us wonder if the fish are dazed by the confusion of waters. We know they are temperature sensitive and the lateral lines on the fish are filled with neuromasts that allow them to detect both weak water motions and pressure gradients.

Downstream, the bluffs rise steeply and provide wonderful mural escarpments of limestone just between their peaks and sandstone on the lower elevations. We saw seven bald eagles, numerous great blue herons, crows, and swirling kettles of turkey vultures as we cruised downstream beside occasional sandy islands of dredge materials.

The most shocking sight was Prairie Island Nuclear Power Plant. No matter where we were, power plants were startling places with ominous-looking silos and a long line of cooling towers with wisps of white steam rising against the background of trees. Prairie Island began operating in 1973 with two nuclear reactors. This is the second nuclear plant along our route—Monticello was the first—and it remains the most controversial of the Minnesota plants because of the storage of spent rods in large steel casks within the Mississippi River floodplain. This storage system was opposed by the environmental and the Prairie Island Mdewakanton Sioux communities, but approved by the state and Nuclear Regulatory Agency.

The Prairie Island band had already lost substantial land to the lock and dam and Corp of Engineers before losing more to the power plant.

We entered lock #3 along with a large tour boat from Treasure Island casino. We slid into the large-capacity lock and grabbed a rope given to us by the lock master. Then the massive doors to the rear closed and the water was released until the level matched the downstream side.

As we entered Red Wing, the parks and marinas were the first sight and then the famous Barn Bluff rose behind the grain towers, railroad yards, and barges. This grand bluff was an island in the Glacial River Warren and thus has a very unique shape that was noted by most early travelers. The bluff itself is made up of ancient oceanic deposits. I used to bring my college students here to see the Red Wing Fault Line near the intersection of Highway 61 and Minnesota 58, where the rocks are displaced 125 feet, putting unrelated eras of rock formation right next to each other. This layer cake of a bluff is a wonderful greenish color in the lower Franconia Formation, caused by the mineral glauconite. The layers going up include the Jordan Sandstone, one of many layers of Cambrian sandstone. These are capped by the stronger layer of Oneota Dolomite, a type of limestone rich in magnesium.

The Mississippian culture—the same great culture that built the mounds of Cahokia near St. Louis—also built mounds in this area, including

some on the bluff. This culture was eventually displaced by the Mdewakan-ton Dakota around 1815. The town gets its name from the Dakota leader known as Red Wing, even though his name according to some historical accounts was actually Walking Buffalo (Tatankamani), which would have made a good community name, too. The Dakota used the 350-foot bluff as a lookout, giving them visual control of many miles of river.

We landed at Levee Park, a stretch of greenway filled with people enjoying the great weather of this June 21 Summer Solstice day. A sailboat named the *Beluga* was at the dock and in front of that was a barge anchored at the grain elevator. We walked across the railroad tracks past the depot, which now includes an art gallery, and up to the historic St. James Hotel, where we had lunch on their veranda, perched up a story from the slanting sidewalk. The town is classic brickwork. Known for shipping and for Red Wing shoes, this is a popular tourist destination.

We sat in the breeze (wind) and sipped our Surly beer and ate our brisket sandwiches. I looked at Barn Bluff and thought about all who have climbed it, including Zebulon Pike, Henry Schoolcraft, and Henry David Thoreau. In *Westward I Go Free* by Corrine Hosfeld Smith, the author says that during their stay in Red Wing, at the Metropolitan Hotel, Henry David Thoreau and Horace Mann were at the base of Barn Bluff and "It was yet another interesting site for two botanists to investigate. They spent many hours over the next three days doing so." Young Horace was most excited about finding *"Pulsatilla Nutalliana* in bloom on top" of Barn Bluff. Thoreau noted that the *Lobelia* was "bluer than common" and Pepper Grass the "commonest weed."

Seeing a large towboat pushing a series of barges upriver caused us to move quickly so we could get to the lock for our upstream trip before it became entangled with the logistics of barges. This allowed us to move past the towboat and watch as it navigated a sharp corner. Barges do not turn—they are pushed where they need to go and the narrow channel and the tight turn were an excellent example of the pilot's skills.

After the lock, we were treated to a bald eagle that sat on a sunken log off the main channel. It was just above water and moved along the log, allowing us great opportunities to observe and enjoy it. Then we came upon another unusual sight. I saw something nearing the shore—Kate insisted they were sticks, which made this a reversal of our deer sighting when we were walking on the Sibley Peninsula during our walk around Lake Superior. But I saw that these sticks were in fact two pair of ears— two deer, swimming side by side, having crossed this large river and now climbing up the wooded islands that dot the Minnesota side from the sediments of the Cannon and Vermilion rivers.

Moving back upstream, we cruised around the Prescott marina, slid under the bridges at Hastings, and cruised up to Lock #2, which was filled with a down-bound set of barges. Under the massive bluff on the east side, a red engine freight train moved along the tracks, and we had an image of the river that was in stark contrast to the small stream we had explored in the north, yet it was still the Mississippi.

Lake Pepin

ALONG THE SHORES of Lake Pepin are Lake City on the Minnesota shore and Pepin on the Wisconsin. Pepin is tucked into the shoreline and more secluded, while Lake City has Highway 61 running between it and the lake, with a marina and parks inviting one to cool off on a hot summer day. The most intriguing thing about this part of the lake is the sign that proclaims Lake City to be the home of waterskiing. Ralph Samuelson is credited as the inventor of the sport. Legend has it Samuelson used staves from wooden barrels and snow skis before he created new skis made of pine boards eight feet long and nine inches wide. June 28, 1922, Samuelson stood on top of an aquaplane board and lowered himself on to the water one foot at a time. Yes—a plane!

Lake Pepin is the last of the large natural lakes, but also a precursor to the big pools upstream of each of the locks. This thirty-mile long lake

lines up with the wind and creates what sailors know as a long fetch. Fetch is defined as the distance over open water that wind moves unimpeded. The longer the fetch, the higher the resultant waves. What seems like a mild condition on the offshore conditions can become a dangerous and life-threatening situation.

The name Pepin is attributed to Father Louis Hennepin, who is said to call it the lake of tears (Pleurs) after watching an Isanti Dakota mourn for the death of the chief's son. Hennepin was a captive of the band at the time and would end up going to Lake Mille Lacs, where the group met Sieur du Luht, who would then take the wayward father with him.

When I canoed the Chippewa River (which feeds into Lake Pepin) years ago, I was amazed by the sand accumulations along its banks and on the bottom. This glacial sediment eventually moves into the Mississippi River, but the Chippewa's current is slowed by the larger river and the sand accumulates in a broad delta. The delta is then dissected by both the continuing flow of the Chippewa and the large flow of the Mississippi, creating deltaic islands—something that happens frequently downstream, with many communities like Wabasha located on these outwashes.

Here the accumulation of sand does one more thing: it constricts the valley of the Mississippi, shunting the water that we see in the lake to a small opening on the Minnesota side. The volume that can make it through this constriction is limited and backs up the Mississippi flow, creating a natural impoundment.

Reads Landing to La Crosse

THE WATERS THAT FLOW from the lake are fast in the narrow channel, giving an advantage to eagles that congregate along the river during the winter. In its heyday, Reads Landing is said to have had twenty-seven hotels, numerous saloons, and a variety of other places of commerce. That was during the peak of river traffic from both the Chippewa River and the Mississippi. Today there is a wonderful micro-brewery/restaurant.

Like so many places along the shore, the names of the original inhabitants are prominent in community and local names—Winona, Red Wing, and Dakota, to name a few. Of the states bordering the river, Mississippi, Minnesota, Wisconsin, Illinois, Iowa, Tennessee, Kentucky, Arkansas, and Missouri are all Native-American-based names—only Louisiana is not (it is named after King Louis XIV). All had thriving Native American populations before the Trail of Tears and the forced exodus of Native American peoples in the south. Louisiana, despite its name, was filled with Native American people. In the book *Unfathomable City*, Monique Verdin writes,

> The Bayougoula (bayou people), Mugulasha (people of the other side), Chitimacha (those living on the grand river/those who have pots), Houma (red), Tangipahoa (corn gatherers), Quinapisa (those who see), Tunica (people), Opelousa (black hair), Biloxi (first people), Pascagoula (bread people), Choctaw, Chapitoula (river people), Atakapa (man-eaters), Acolapissa (those who look out for the people), Waha (wandering people of the sea coast/hunting place), Chawasha (raccoon place)—these and many other forgotten Mississippi Delta tribes and names were recorded in the logs of early explorers, settlers, and surveyors and in the journals of Jesuit priests. Oral stories were forgotten when the native languages died, leaving it to imaginations to ponder blurred legacies and lore. Much remains a mystery, lost in translation and left out of historical texts.

Yet the river is conspicuous for the lack of reservations. We encountered reservations canoeing in the northern reaches of the river (Leech

Lake and Prairie Island in Minnesota), but the rest of the river lacks Native American lands. How can this be?

Wabasha is named for Native American chief Wah-pah-sha. We have been there many times over the years. The National Eagle Center is a great location for celebrating the history and presence of our national bird—something I saw almost every day along the river—and the center maintains a volunteer group that keeps us apprised of the population concentrations during the winter.

In this area one summer, I led a group of teachers on a mollusk survey. There are still remnants of the old button factories in towns like Bellevue, Iowa, that prospered from the Mississippi's great variety of mussels. We walked in one of the river's shallow branches, feeling for the mussels with our feet and then bringing them up to identify them. We found ten species during our efforts. A nice sample, but that is a far cry from the 300 species that supposedly still exist.

We know so little about mussels because they are sedentary. We often notice the empty shells from the feeding of muskrat, otter, and raccoon, but not the camouflaged shells of the live filter feeders. Their names alone should elicit our attention: fat pocketbook, pink heel-splitter, three-horn warty back, fatmucket, monkeyface, and wabash pigtoe. The U.S. Fish and Wildlife Service write on their website,

> In North America, it is estimated that forty-three percent of the 300 species of freshwater mussels are in danger of extinction. Further, the current extinction rate (percent loss per decade) for freshwater mussels is 1.2% and is estimated to be 6.4% in the future. These rates fall within the range of estimates for tropical rainforest communities (1-8% loss per decade). Historically, the Midwest boasted the most diverse collection of mussels in the world. But today, the states of Minnesota, Wisconsin, Iowa, Missouri, Illinois, Indiana, and Ohio list more than half of their seventy-eight known mussel species as endangered, threatened, or requiring special concern."

These mussels may only move a few feet in their feeding, but they have some amazing adaptations, like mimicking minnows with the tissue that exudes from their mantle. The feeding fish in the river (they all have a preferred species) come to investigate the potential food and get a spray of eggs in their gills. It is within the fish that the young mussels will develop before dropping back to the river bottom.

The other fascinating fact is that these mussels can live between ten and one hundred years! And, of course, I wondered what made a mussel a "mussel" and not a clam—the best answer I could get other than the difference in taste was that mussels are more elongated members of the clam group.

The use of mussels for buttons was developed by a man named Johann Böpple in 1899, and ten years later there were sixty button factories along the river, with much overharvesting that led to the decline of species and numbers. Later the mussels would be isolated by locks and dams—sometimes excluding the fish species needed for propagation of young. Now the major threat to the native mussels is the zebra mussel, a scourge introduced into the Great Lakes and spreading throughout northern waters.

Alma, Wisconsin, is the next river town and it, like Wabasha, was host to a canoe trip that Kate and I led with Russian and American high school students. This trip had a lot of memories for us, but none more pleasant than when we were met at the Wabasha Park for a picnic and tour of the city, or at the dock in Alma where citizens not only shared their picturesque city but also took us to the top of the bluff and to apple farms where we could taste the bounty of the Mississippi River apples.

This area is wonderful for apples with my favorites, Haralson and Honeycrisp, among the many varieties and flavors that grow in the scenic region. Orchardists in the region are attempting to create their own regional brand, according to *Fruit Grower's News*. Makes sense to me. I had a Honeycrisp every day on the boat during this section of the river.

Just below the Alma lock and dam, we were camped on a sand island and had settled in for a nice evening when the lock opened and a barge and tow emerged. As we watched it suddenly occurred to us that it was not turning. It is a difficult turn since the tow boats have no momentum coming out of the lock and they have to make a right curve. In this case we were startled by a loud crack as the barge hit the shoreline and broke trees as it forced its way around the corner and on downstream: A good lesson on why to camp on the inside of curves.

Winona is below Lock and Dam #5a—the only lock with a letter designation, meaning it was not part of the original plan. Oops. The town is named for chief Wah-pah-sha's daughter—a nice gesture since it was the original site of their village.

Their annual Steamboat Days festival celebrates the city's relationship to the river. The city was the fourth-largest grain distributor in the United States by 1870, and the riverfront today is a blend of parks and industry. I like to visit the Watkin's corporate headquarters for its unique architecture, but also for its museum, where I can see the history of their products and one of the horse-drawn wagons that their salesmen drove—including my Grandfather Link, who acquired the nickname "Doc" from this experience.

The famous Sugar Loaf rock formation on the skyline is actually the remnants of a limestone quarry left in the shape we see today by request to the quarry owner. The person liked the look of it and because of his request we can all enjoy this unusual landmark.

When I left the park in Winona in my small boat, it was October 21. I was disappointed that the river bottoms were not ablaze with color— the reason I left this portion for the autumn, but climatic changes have been affecting the coloring and leaf fall throughout Minnesota. Added to this was the fact that a cold system chose to come out of the mountains and I had snowflakes along with the wind.

It was a lead-gray sky as I passed under the bridges and past the plants that make up Winona. The wind at my back added some speed, but also added some worry to my trip downstream. Cruising south, I found myself in large open stretches with lots of floating vegetation that had been set loose by either boats or wind and my little fifteen-horse motor would groan, necessitating that I back off the prop and clear the vegetation before moving on. All this was complicated by the waves.

As I came up on Trempealeau I was excited to see Trempealeau and Perrot "mountains" with their unique goat prairies on their flanks. My pleasure was short-lived. The winds from the broad pool (reservoir) above the lock and dam were accumulating more height and as I came up on the lock I realized they were also bounding off the lock and creating a confused sea that intensified their height with added unpredictability. My

swirling little boat seemed even smaller as I tried to hold my position until
the lock could open. I was happy to get through and have the dam block
the wind and waves again.

Finally I came to Dresbach, and then La Crosse Lock and Dam #7. A
barge was about to enter the lock, meaning I would have hours to wait. I
was really cold; the light snow, strong winds, wave spray and a high of
thirty-nine degrees made me highly hypothermic, and I knew I would need
to get warm. I pulled off at the Dresbach landing and got out my phone. My
plan was to stay at the home of our friends Dr. Doug and Teresa White in
Onalaska, and luckily for me Doug was able to come to the landing, had a
boat trailer, and welcomed me to his home for dinner, brews, and a warm
bed. Here Jon Soul would join me for the next three days of travel.

Great friendship makes a memorable evening. Doug had been a
camp guide at the Audubon Center that I directed in Sandstone, Minnesota, and he had joined Kate and me for sailing on Lake Superior. Jon
(pronounced Yon) Soul was also at the Audubon Center as an intern, but
his route was a little different. He was working on a paddlewheeler in
1991 that Kate and I were on for a writing assignment. In the evenings

he and I talked about how he got on the boat, what he wanted to do, and finally departed with him saying, "If you need any bags carried, let me know." I said I had canoes that needed portaging and when he was ready, he should call me. And he did! Thus began a long and wonderful friendship. He now lives in Shreveport, Louisiana, where he works in a Montessori school and coordinates a program called B2B—Bayou to Bay—that has taken the local bayou and brought it to the attention of the community, schools, and teachers. He runs workshops on watershed education after canoeing from the cement drainage system to the Gulf of Mexico. The upper part of the river is where we met, and this would be an excellent place for us to have another adventure together.

La Crosse to Prairie du Chien

JON AND I LEFT La Crosse via the Black River on a gorgeous morning; such a nice change from the gray and windy experiences upstream. We had an easy morning with a large Army Corp of Engineers dredge in one location, bridge work in Lansing, Iowa, and a few swans and egrets along the islands. Two bald eagles shared a signal light at one bend and other eagles

continued to entertain us, but most of all we were absorbed by the landscape of river bluffs with their tan mural escarpments contrasting with
the green and colored leaves.

We had our next adventure near Genoa (named for Christopher
Columbus's hometown by Italian immigrants), which was originally the
village of Bad Axe—a name I prefer. The steamboat landing, hotels, and
dance halls are no longer here and the setting is just a peaceful village
with a railroad track and highway between the water's edge and bluff. We
were racing to get ahead of a barge and tow—something that could cost
us two to four hours of waiting. We were also trying to avoid the floating
mats of vegetation that would clog the small motor's props when we
sighted a log with ears pass in front of us. Another deer had decided to
cross the river where there was a mile of open water. We floated up toward it and it kept swimming to the shore where it climbed out, shaking
off the water as it ran up the embankment, across the railroad tracks,
jumped over the guardrail, and ran across the road to the bluff.

The lock master agreed to let us go to the front of the lock and the
barges were brought in behind us. Talk about feeling small. The three
wide barges filled the lock and towered over us. We watched and tried
not to think about the fact that they did not have brakes. The tow operator

knew what to do, and it was a safe exit for us out in front of the towboat and past the coal plant on the Wisconsin shore.

Crossing the Iowa line meant we would be leaving the Minnesota portion of the river—just shy of 1,000 miles of Mississippi River waters are in or along the state of Minnesota. Just below this border is Battle Island, which in my opinion is very misnamed. It should be "Massacre Island," because it was here that Blackhawk's rear guard was caught by an armed steamboat and the militia. Driven off the island over 150 Native Americans—men, women, children—were killed or drowned, and another fifty captured. Three hundred made it across the river only to be killed by Dakota under the instigation of General Atkinson. It is a truly sad place on a river that has had many heart-rending floods, fires, earthquakes, and wars. The next bridge at Lansing is named Blackhawk Bridge—I'm not sure the great chief would be honored.

Lansing sits between large river bluffs with Hosmer Bluff overlook peering into three converging states. The bluff is named for the American sculptor Harriet Hosmer, who supposedly climbed the bluff in 1851. People now drive to the top—hardly the same experience.

The next community of note is Lynxville, Wisconsin. I love the setting and of course I like the name, although I do prefer "Link" to "Lynx." At

Lynxville we got to Lock and Dam #9. The clouds were coming back and the temperature was dropping. Our great day was starting to resemble our previous weather.

Below the lock on the Iowa side is a large bluff I visited many times with family and college students, Effigy Mounds National Monument. The monument website gives this explanation for the mounds:

> The Late Woodland Period (1400–750 B.P.) along the Upper Mississippi River and extending east to Lake Michigan is associated with the culture known today as the Effigy Moundbuilders. The construction of effigy mounds was a regional cultural phenomenon. Mounds of earth in the shapes of birds, bear, deer, bison, lynx, turtle, panther, or water spirit are the most common images. Like earlier groups, the Effigy Moundbuilders continued to build conical mounds for burial purposes, but their burial sites lacked the trade goods of the preceding Middle Woodland Culture. The Effigy Moundbuilders also built linear or long rectangular mounds used for ceremonial purposes that remain a mystery. Some archeologists believe they were built to mark celestial events or seasonal observances. Others speculate they were constructed as territorial markers or as boundaries between groups.

The animal-shaped mounds remain the symbol of the Effigy Mounds Culture. Along the Mississippi River in northeast Iowa and across the river in southwest Wisconsin, two major animal mound shapes seem to prevail: the bear and the bird. Near Lakes Michigan and Winnebago, water spirit earthworks—historically called turtle and panther mounds—are more common.

Dusk was approaching, the temperatures were quickly dropping into the low thirties, and the wind was picking up again. We took the channel to Prairie du Chien, where we intended to camp. There was a nice dock and we came up the stairs to Lawler Park, but camping did not seem likely. We saw a pavilion, picnic tables, and a nice trail with excellent signs, but no campsites. We should have been in the right place since this was the historic landing for voyageur canoes, but it was not used as such now.

The city's website claims it is the oldest European-settled city on the upper Mississippi. Prairie du Chien is located just above the Mississippi's confluence with the Wisconsin River and was the location for Fort Crawford (British), Villa Louis (the mansion of the fur baron Hercules Dousman), and Fort Shelby (American). The town history is like a "who's who"

list; besides Dousman, there was the visit by Marquette and Jolliet, who kicked off the European invasion.

Famous residents also include Dr. Beaumont. He was an army surgeon who had a patient with a wound that would not close over, giving the doctor a chance to observe and take notes on our gastric physiology. The voyageur Alexis St. Martin first came to the doctor on Mackinac Island with a hole caused by a musket ball. In 1829, the doctor was transferred to Fort Crawford and brought Alexis in as a servant so he could continue to study the man's digestive system. Martin would follow Beaumont to Washington, D.C., where the doctor would continue to put different items into his patient's stomach and observe what happened. Martin lived fifty-eight years after the initial wound and moved back to Canada, where he lived as a farmer.

In addition, the roll of names includes Blackhawk, the warrior who surrendered at Fort Crawford to future president Zachary Taylor, John Lawler, who is famed for his philanthropy, Buffalo Bill, who rode into town on his famous steed to quell a fight between his performers and some local citizens, and of course there were steamboats, canoes, barges, and who knows how many others who found shelter in Prairie du Chien, as we intended to do.

Across the trail, road, and railroad tracks was the Depot Bar. We sauntered over (I always wanted to use "saunter" since my love affair with westerns as a kid) and entered the bar to ask if they knew if we could camp in the park. The answer was no. Since we had been slightly hypothermic and shaking from the wind and cold, the disappointment must have been quite obvious. The manager of the bar came to our rescue. "The bar is private property—you can camp here," he told us. So with that turn of events we set up our tents outside the bar, quite close to the railroad tracks—we had not paid enough attention to how many trains had passed us as we came south on the river, but we would be reminded all night long.

But first things first—we needed liquid, something hot to eat, and a place to warm up. The Depot did it for us. It was established in this spot in 1864 and had been upgraded since then, but still had the look and feel of an old-fashioned depot. In our tents, we felt the temperature drop to twenty-three degrees that night—and freezing rain was followed by snow. My shoulders were fully enraged and would not let me sleep during much of the night, and when I did doze off, a train would come by with horns and vibrations that made sure I would have to push an internal reset to get rest.

In the morning, our breakfast under the pavilion roof was a pleasant affair except that the Coleman fuel canisters froze up and had to be warmed by hand before restarting. We tried to do this quickly before we lost the heat that had already been absorbed by the water. We also found ourselves the curiosity of the day with cars coming by to check us out, including one driven by Donna Reed, who found us fascinating and just wanted to talk to us and share her story. She told us about her dad, who had done a lot of archaeology in the area and insisted that she show one of us the first river dredge that was now at the museum. I sent Jon and watched the gear and the stove.

Prairie du Chien to Dubuque

DU CHIEN MEANS DOG—the French translation of the name of the Sauk Indian chief who lived here. It made me think about Lucas Will, who was at that moment canoeing the river with his dog Tischer. Many people have heard of the musical group Three Dog Night and how they got their name from the description of how many dogs were needed to keep a person warm along the trail. I suspect that Tischer had not been warm enough for Lucas during the previous night.

The Wisconsin River, which feeds into the Mississippi in this area, was the route for early explorers and was also the river John Muir floated when he was a student at the University of Wisconsin. It is a massive flow with lots of sediment that forms the islands beneath Wyalusing State Park, an excellent park I have enjoyed exploring in the past. I could not help but remember one adventure when I was in the backwaters with my rubber raft and had to fend off two banded watersnakes that seemed intent on joining me. My biggest concern was keeping them from striking the raft as I pushed them away.

Silica mines have been in this region for a long time—one mine was started in 1878—and as we started out we could see the rail cars filled with the lime. There were barges and trucks in the area of one mine where we were startled by a truck driving out of a cave beneath a cliff. The wind was cool again today with the temperature in the high thirties, and we saw only a few good birds along the river.

We found our way past a barge-and-tow combination through the twisted course in the McMillan Island complex, a route difficult for barge-

and-tow operations because they had to gain power after leaving the Guttenberg Lock, then turn their load multiple times in a short and narrow channel. We slid past the outside channel markers and rode out the waves.

Guttenberg is a fascinating community named for the person who invented the movable clay printing press in 1041. Using moveable wooden print blocks, he is responsible for the creation of books and is one of the most important inventors in history. However, the town, while named for him, shows that errors do occur in printing and thus the town name misspells his name—which is Gutenberg.

We watched a school class marching toward Lock and Dam #10 as we slid in and were lowered during a snow flurry.

The cold came with the snow, and we were chilled again (I was shaking) as we moved toward Cassville, one of the oldest towns in Wisconsin. We were forced to leave the river for a warm up and chose to get out of the increasing winds and buy a lunch at the local Crossroads Café, where we enjoyed good food in a relaxed atmosphere with Andy Griffith and Barney Fife playing on the black-and-white TV. It could not have been a better combination. We were given great hospitality and food. They closed at 2:00 P.M., though, so we were inspired to go back on the river and continue our journey.

Our big issue was the gas tank. The places we thought we could get gas were closed for the season, and we continued on in hope we would not face big waves or long delays that might eat into the remaining fuel. If all went well, we were good.

Following our charts, we were measuring progress against the buoys and channel lights and markers. Doing this allowed us a chance to enjoy the creative names and wonder how they were given. For example, there was Milkman's Light, French Light, Hanging Rock Light, Lost Slough, Deadman's Slough, and others that invoked images but told us no tales.

Wind and waves built up as we moved south of Rosebrook Island Light and into the exposed pool above Lock and Dam #11. We were watching for places to pull off if the conditions got too bad. The fetch for this open water area was eleven miles and the navigational channel twists and turns across the pool, following the old river channel. Our little boat was exposed to waves from multiple directions.

We were fortunate to make it through the lock without any delays, but because our fuel was getting low we chose to go to the city dock in

Dubuque near the National Mississippi River Museum and Aquarium. The port offices were closed and fuel was not available for the evening. In addition, we knew the gate would lock behind us and we would have no way to get back to our boat. Jon and I tied it off and knew we could not camp here, so we worked together to get our essential gear to the gate. Then we went out and got a room, expecting to get gas in the morning.

However, in the morning the offices did not open until 10:00 A.M. and no one around the docks could help us. Many tried, using codes they thought would work, but we wanted to get back on the water. Even the temptation of the aquarium, where I have brought college classes in the past, was not enough to satisfy us. When a canoeist arrived and came up through the gate we took advantage and got back to our boat and across to East Dubuque, where we had learned the marina was open and had gasoline.

It was too brief a visit to Dubuque. The town is one of the most vibrant on the river and the aquarium is rivaled only by the New Orleans Aquarium. The red brick buildings and the towers on top of the buildings make for a great skyline as we traveled in and out of the community on this trip.

Dubuque to Clinton, Iowa

COLD WEATHER AND WIND continued to buffet us as we traveled south from Dubuque. One highlight was the sight of the *Queen of the Mississippi*—the same boat I had traveled the southern portion of the river on and on which Kate and I work as Riverlorians. We saw it in the distance, and I was able to gain contact with Captain Trabor on the marine band radio. He did not come out and wave—they had brushed an inch of snow off the decks in the morning and it was too cold to be that social.

Galena, Iowa, was once an important part of the Mississippi steamboat trade, but the Galena River can no longer support the large boats that accessed the community nor the lead that gave the community both its name and its economy. Lead demand died down and the river trade moved elsewhere. Now the town is one of the most historic of river cities and people flock here to walk the streets, shop, and explore the sense of history both downtown and at Ulysses S. Grant's home. This was where he began his military career, culminating in being elected to the presidency of the United States.

Across the wide, shallow pool was the Potosi Landing, but it was not on our schedule. Potosi is not next to the river. It is in a proverbial hollow, a wonderful place where valleys converge in the bluff country. To reach it, Kate and I went by car on a separate trip. The nearest larger town is Dickeyville, best known for the grotto next to the Holy Ghost Parish. Built from 1925 to 1931 by Father Matthias Wernerus, the site is described on the Grotto's webpage thus:

> It is a creation in stone, mortar, and bright-colored objects—collected materials from all over the world. These include colored glass, gems, antique heirlooms of pottery or porcelain, stalagmites and stalactites, sea shells, starfish, petrified sea urchins and fossils, and a variety of corals, amber glass, agate, quartz, ores such as iron, copper and lead, fool's gold, rock crystals, onyx, amethyst and coal, petrified wood, and moss.

The spirits of Potosi are quite different and very popular based on the crowds encountered at the restaurant, bar, and museum that are the centerpiece of the Potosi Brewing Company complex. Originally started in 1852, the brewery, like so many throughout Wisconsin, succumbed to prohibition. But a young set of entrepreneurs established it again in 2008, and their quality beer has become a cause of celebration and expansion.

The brewery building is old-style river brick and the little area around the brewery is lively and scenic. But best of all, the food and the beer are exceptional. It is definitely one of the places that earn the sobriquet "off the beaten path" or "hidden gem."

Back on the river, our goal was Bellevue, Iowa, by noon to meet Kate and her friend Karen for lunch. Bellevue Landing, below the lock and dam, was next to the old button factory. The landing was full of boats going to fish for walleye below the dam. We were happy to land and get out of the wind. Kate brought us lunch from her mom, and we enjoyed sandwiches in an open gazebo ("enjoyed" might be stretching things, as Karen thought she would freeze to death). Jon bid farewell at this point. Karen would drive him to his car, and Kate would pick up our truck. I was now on my own.

I went downtown to get a hot cup of coffee to drink on my cold and windy trip. The button factory was soon behind me and all that I took from Bellevue was the story of the 1840 gun battle that seemed more dramatic than the OK Corral in Tombstone. It seems that a gang of murderers and livestock rustlers came to town and conducted mayhem, but did not get away. Instead, they were quickly captured and subjected to a democratic justice—a vote of the citizens to hang them or make them go away. They were saved by the vote and put on a raft and sent downriver without a paddle. This would have been good riddance except that they came ashore in Davenport and killed an innocent man.

The wind would be my companion and it was still strong. I managed to enjoy the river, although one more paddlewheeler was sending up a big wake and not giving up any part of the channel. The *Starlight* was obviously on its way someplace and it was the biggest wake I had to ride out.

Palisades State Park is a place I had camped as I explored the river when writing our *Grandparents Illinois Style* book. I loved the high overlook that let me see up and down the river. This time I enjoyed seeing the cliffs that give the park its name.

Downriver from Palisades was Sabula, Iowa. Kate and I had to return by vehicle to explore it. Only 1.26 square miles in size, with .40 square miles of that above water, this is Iowa's only island city. It is connected to land by causeways, one of which leads to the bridge that connects with Savanna, Illinois. The small town fills the island and has a history of fishing, logging, buttons, and meat packing. That is a lot of industry for a small plot of land that has to have suffered from a lot of floods over the decades. Today it is primarily a place for recreational fishing.

From there to Lock and Dam #13, the pool is large and the wind, heavy all day, had the waters churned up. I tried to get ahead of two barge-tow units without taking on too much water, and I was successful in getting to the lock ahead of them. My problem was that the lock was filled with fueling Army Corp boats. I had to wait while the waves built and

rushed from the north, then hit the lock, dam, and breakwater and re-
bounded into the oncoming waves. The confused seas reached frothy
peaks, and the boat wanted to settle backward in to the water, which
would have slid my little motor in. I had to give it some fuel, and then
when I went over a crest it wanted to rush in to the next wave. I took on
some water and bounced in the turbulent water until I heard the lock
master tell the Corps he had to get the little boat out of the waves and
into shelter, words that warmed my heart.

They opened the doors and I came in behind the barges and boats
of the Corps. When the doors closed behind me the seas calmed and I took
a breath. Then when the front doors opened a Corps person on their boat
told me to "hit it"—he waved me around the boat and down a corridor
where I had a foot and a half to spare on each side of the boat between
the wall and the barge. "Give it some gas," he yelled, and I did.

The dam removed the waves and blocked the wind so I could float
slowly down the river between the old logging town of Clinton, Iowa, and
the Illinois city of Fulton, with its Dutch windmill next to the levee. This
Dutch village is also where the Lincoln Highway (Highway 30) crosses

from Illinois to Iowa. The Lincoln Highway is famous for being the first transcontinental highway in the United States and was dedicated in 1913. It was also the first national memorial for Abraham Lincoln, predating the Lincoln monument.

At Clinton, I went to the dock inside the floodwall and tied off. Kate would be coming to join me, but it would be three to four hours. I walked the town and visited the courthouse, which is one of most impressive on the river. I walked the park and the levee and sat with my boat until it got dark. Then I went to the marina bar and waited until Kate called.

We got a room for the night and I planned my next day. The temperature dropped into the mid-twenties, and I was expecting to get up and head downriver, but things conspired to change those plans.

First was the weather prediction of winds howling down the river at thirty miles per hour—which would exceed what I could handle in my small boat. Second, my back and shoulders did not allow me to sleep. Two inflamed shoulders combined with the spinal injuries in my neck and what I would later learn was ulnar neuropathy in each elbow and carpal tunnel in each wrist kept me from relaxing and dozing off for more than sporadic sleep. The third factor was that Kate was there, and she knew I needed to quit the river. I had now gone from Itasca to Clinton and from St. Louis to the Gulf of Mexico, but the stretch ahead of me was not going to work—the extended weather picture did not have any break coming for the next week, and I did not have the money to wait it out. So this was the end of the northern portion of the river and the primary floating for the year, except for two more weeks on the southern section. Luckily, I would be on a big boat for this section the next year.

Clinton to St. Louis

I MIGHT NOT HAVE been able to paddle this section, but that didn't stop us from exploring it by car on a different trip. Le Claire, Iowa, is a small town with a main street that parallels the river and the railroad. One of the fascinating surprises was the Buffalo Bill Cody Museum located in the *Lone*

Star towboat—the last wooden-hulled paddlewheel boat that remains intact. This is Buffalo Bill's birthplace, an event that took place in the same year that Iowa became a state. His homestead cabin is no longer here, moved by rail to Cody, Wyoming, but the setting is still an inspiring.

Le Claire is at the head of the Rock Island Rapids. It was first settled by a *metis* (mixed blood) trader named Le Claire who knew the Upper Rock Island Rapids would stop many travelers. Two enterprising men named Smith and Suiter decided to study the rapids, boils, eddies, and obstacles and prepared themselves for a career as rapids pilots. In 1877, a canal around the rapids put the twenty men then working as pilots out of business. Later, the rock would be blasted and removed, making this another stretch of calm navigable water—except when the south wind blows the surface water and makes the river look like it is heading back to Itasca.

Approaching Bettendorf, one of the quad cities, there is a large building on the hillside called the Abbey Hotel. It was built in 1917 for the Sisters of Our Lady of Mount Carmel, and is hard to miss. Bettendorf is named for the axle manufacturer, who moved his business to what was then known as Gilbertown.

Moline, on the Illinois side, is the home of John Deere manufacturing. Besides having the John Deere name all over the area, it has a series of museums and shops where we brought our grandson Matthew to explore. He was five years old and the tractors in the pavilion were gigantic, but he managed to climb in and out of them and enjoy the spectacle, while his grandfather found the shop and collection of antique tractors fascinating. From there to the city docks was an easy walk, and he and Kate fed the ducks while we talked about the river. Originally the town was called Milltown or Rock Island Mills, but the name did not seem to resonate so another was sought. They considered Hesperia, but switched to Moline from the French word *moulin* (which meant mill), and the name stuck.

Arsenal Island was a prisoner of war camp for Confederate soldiers, with as many as 12,000 held here. Originally called Fort Armstrong, the first fort was dismantled and put under the command of George Davenport. When the Civil War began, the site was chosen to be an arsenal.

Lock and Dam #15 was built at the foot of the Rock Island Rapids, and its pool inundated the historic stretch of difficult water. Below the lock is the double-decker bridge that carries both cars and railroad trains

across the Mississippi. It is the second double-decker in the area. Bridges are part of the history of the quad cities; the first railroad bridge to span the river is just upstream from the current bridge. Much to the dismay of the steamboat operators, this bridge was intended to connect the Chicago and Rock Island Railroad with the newly created Mississippi and Missouri railroads. Just to add intrigue to controversy, the steamer *Effie Afton* hit the bridge, destroying both the steamer and one of the spans on May 6, 1856. Jefferson Davis, who would become the president of the Confederacy, was in favor of the bridge until he saw that it was not connecting the southern states to the west. With all this tension swirling around, the railroads had to hire a lawyer for a case that would go all the way to the Supreme Court—the lawyer was from Illinois, named Abraham Lincoln.

Davenport was originally called Morgan's Camp by the Native Americans and Stubb's Eddy by the rivermen. Colonel Davenport of Rock Island bought seven-eighths of the land that would become the city from Antoine LeClaire, from whom the town just north gets its name. The final city of the "quad" is Rock Island, which was evidently a quite subdued community, considering that they passed laws forbidding horse racing, gambling, firecrackers, "Hallooing," shouting, bawling, screaming, and obscene language. Originally called Stephenson, the city changed its name to Rock Island in 1841. Just south of the town is the Rock River, where former president Ronald Reagan worked as a lifeguard. For what it's worth, this is the first place we encountered Maid-Rite restaurants, which specialize in a "loose" hamburger—the franchise began in Quincy, Illinois.

Muscatine, the next city of size on the river, had a brief reign as the pearl button capitol of the world. Over half of the citizens worked in one of the forty-three button factories. Hard to imagine! Originally the town was called Bloomington, but all their mail was going to Illinois or Indiana, so they changed it. So far as we can tell, it is the only Muscatine in the world—an amazing fact considering how names are reused. Of course, the translation of the name is not certain. Suggestions include "fiery nation," "burning island," and "people of the prairie." Still others say it is the name of the Mascouten Indians.

The Iowa River enters the Mississippi across from New Boston, Illinois. The river is 323 miles long and passes the University at Iowa City, where we once canoed the muddy waters.

Burlington, Iowa, was named after a Vermont city at the suggestion of the first citizen to buy a lot in the town. It is one of numerous Iowan cities located next to the river—for some reason, Illinois does not have the same size and abundance of river towns. Below Burlington is the 1928 Highway 9/Railroad Bridge, which has 525-foot swingspan. This double-decked bridge is one the most impressive on the river.

One prominent city on the Illinois side of the river is Nauvoo. The name is supposed to be an Anglicized version of a Hebrew name meaning "to be beautiful." The community was renamed by Joseph Smith after the Mormons (today known as the Church of Jesus Christ of Latter-day Saints) purchased the town of Commerce and made this their religious and community center. The community was first named Quashquema, the name of the local Sauk and Fox leader, was changed to Venus in 1829 when it became large enough to have a post office, and changed again in 1834 to Commerce. Today the old Mormon homes are incorporated into an historic district with tours and a visitor museum. Up the hill is the Mormon temple and statues of Brigham Young and Joseph Smith on horseback looking at the river.

The Mormons were forced from Nauvoo and crossed the Mississippi on flat boats with ends that folded up for the float and dropped down for landing. A nice example is in the park, with a Conestoga wagon covering most of the raft.

Meandering

Keokuk is the last Mississippi River city in Iowa and is just above the confluence of the Des Moines River, which is 525 miles long and begins in Minnesota. Once again, the city is named for a Native American chief. Across the river from Keokuk is Warsaw, Illinois, the hometown to Lincoln's private secretary John Hay. Hay also served as Secretary of State for presidents William McKinley and Theodore Roosevelt. We found the Warsaw Brewing Company in the old brewery ruins near the shore of the Mississippi and thought it was a great setting for sipping and watching the river go by.

Quincy, Illinois, was settled by John Wood, who came west from Moravia, New York, in 1818. He put down roots on Native American land that had been set aside for veterans of the War of 1812. Originally called Bluffs, the town takes its name from President John Quincy Adams. This community was an important part of the Underground Railroad, and the Civil War monument is located high on the bluff at the most picturesque cemetery that we found on the one roadtrip. The old headstones sit among old trees overlooking the Mississippi.

Hannibal, Missouri, sits on the Mississippi south of a large bluff with statues of Tom Sawyer and Huck Finn standing below the slope. This is the town of Samuel Clemens, also known as Mark Twain. It is the site where the Mississippi River and the characters in the town inspired the biography of two of the most famous fictitious young boys in the history of literature. The author left Hannibal when he was seventeen to work as a riverboat pilot.

Today you can find the fence Tom Sawyer whitewashed and the homes of the people who inspired the books. With the flow of immigrants, the constant docking of steamboats, the logging, and the activity of a bustling town, Clemens had inspiration for a lifetime. There are Mark Twain signs and stores to satisfy the pilgrims and a view from the blufftop to see what this section of river looks like.

Downstream is Jackson Island, which many people believe is the place he wrote of in *Huckleberry Finn*, chapters seven through nine. My river chart does not name it, but instead has Shuck Island—maybe "Shuck" and "Huck" is a clue. Jackson is the island where Huck hid out after faking his death. He was there for three days before discovering the slave Jim and formulating the friendship that would carry the novel. It is also a place important for its natural landscape, the idyllic refuge from the pressures of human society. Most importantly, one should not visit without reading something by Mark Twain while there.

Louisiana, Missouri, has a great bluff from which to view the river and an impressive bridge, but the most enjoyable aspect is the name—Louisiana. John Walter Bayse, the founder, named the town in 1817 after his daughter, Louisiana Bayse (this story is disputed, and so are all the other explanations, but I like this best). In case one wonders about a town with another state's name, think about Samuel Clemens—he was not born in Hannibal, but in Florida, Missouri.

The Missouri Department of Natural Resources says Louisiana has "the most intact Victorian streetscape in the state of Missouri." Before the bridges, the river ferry was a "hayburner," that is, a ferry fueled by a horse forced to walk paddlewheels that turned the side wheels and propelled the craft. This would be the aquatic version of a Stairmaster.

The mouth of the Illinois River comes in at Grafton, Illinois. This river is the water route to Chicago, but in recent years has become infamous for the infestation of Asian carp. The Illinois River, with the city of Chicago's canal, ties Lake Michigan to the Great River.

Grafton suffered greatly from a flood in 1993—over one-third of the citizens left town. The historic 1927 flood was terrible by every measurement, but the 1993 flood exceeded the level and damage of twenty-seven feet. What made it doubly difficult for Grafton was the fact that the Illinois River was also in flood stage.

Portage Des Sioux was a shortcut to the Missouri, and the Native Americans chose to cover the two miles overland distance between the Missouri and the Mississippi by carrying their boats rather than making the longer paddle of twenty-five miles. Now there is a yacht club at the portage. In 1951, the Missouri River broke through the St. Charles levee, flooding this community from the west. The pastor of the St. Francis Church called his parishioners to prayer and directed them to the statue of Mary, giving her a new name—Our Lady of Rivers. After two weeks, when the waters receded without destroying their homes, it became a shrine. Annually, there is a blessing of the fleet in July. She even withstood the 1993 flood.

Downstream is a very different shrine—the Piasa Bird! This is perhaps the most unusual marking, shrine, or artwork on the river and the only way to tell about it is to quote from the town of Alton, Illinois's, website about it.

> The Piasa Bird (pronounced Pie-a-saw), is a local legend in the Alton area. Its foundings go back to 1673, when Father Jacques Marquette, in recording his famous journey down the Mississippi River with Louis Joliet, described the "Piasa" as a birdlike monster painted high on the bluffs along the Mississippi River, where the city of Alton, Illinois, now stands.
>
> Father Marquette wrote this description, "While Skirting some rocks, which by Their height and length inspired awe, We saw upon one of them two painted monsters which at first made Us afraid, and upon Which the boldest savages dare not Long rest their eyes. They are as large As a calf; they have Horns on their heads Like those of a deer, a horrible look, red eyes, a beard Like a tiger's, a face somewhat like a man's, a body Covered with scales, and so Long A tail that it winds all around the Body, passing above the head and going back between the legs, ending in a Fish's tail. Green, red, and black are the three Colors composing the Picture. Moreover, these two monsters are so well painted that we cannot believe that any savage is their author; for good painters in France would find it difficult to reach that place conveniently to paint them."

Thanks to civic pride, the bird has been repainted and resides in all its splendor for more generations of river travelers. It is only fitting, since legend has it surviving from the time of mastodons. Just south of the big bird is Alton, which was a key location on the Underground Railroad. If one had been on the river at the right time, that person might have seen slaves crossing and then moving north while Confederate soldiers might have been swimming to Missouri to escape the Union prison in Illinois.

Almost as famous as the Piasa was the gentle giant Robert Pershing Wadlow, who died at age twenty-two and was then recorded to be eight feet, eleven inches tall. It was an unfortunate condition, but he was reputed to be a wonderful person and there is a statue of him in Alton. The musicians Miles Davis and Douglas Wood, author of the classic children's book *Old Turtle*, were also born in Alton.

The Melvin Price Lock and Dam #26 finishes the series of locks and dams on the Mississippi. On the Illinois side, it includes the hands-on River Museum and a biking trail. On the Missouri side, in West Alton, is the Audubon Center at Riverlands, a unique partnership between the National Audubon Society and the Army Corps of Engineers. Riverlands Migratory Bird Sanctuary has trails, interpretive staff, and exhibits and is just upstream from the junction of the Missouri and Mississippi Rivers.

This is the beginning of the St. Louis metro area, with the unique Gateway Arch poised on the hill above the riverfront. Here are numerous bridges, a bike trail that crosses between Illinois and Missouri, and many junctions with the Underground Railroad, the Trail of Tears, the Lewis and Clark Expedition, and the commerce of riverboats, railroads, and highways.

Chapter Eight

The Middle Mississippi

MIKE

St. Louis to Cairo and the Ohio River

THE MIDDLE MISSISSIPPI is not an official designation. The Army Corps of Engineers has charts for the upper and lower Mississippi, with Memphis as the middle ground. But that makes no sense except in their district divisions. The true upper Mississippi goes from Itasca to Minneapolis, after which it becomes the river of commerce and locks that extend down to the Missouri River. This section has a geological affinity. The lower Mississippi is defined by the point where the Ohio River enters. That leaves the distinct section where the Missouri River is the dominant water to the point where the waters of the Ohio double the stream flow again—what people call the middle Mississippi.

If the first is defined by lakes and small dams, the second section of the river, from Minneapolis to the Missouri, is defined by locks and dams. In the middle section, the water flows freely within a natural valley until the Ohio. The fourth section loses the natural valley, and locks and dams are replaced by levees, wing dams, and battures.

Travel from St. Louis to Memphis was on the paddlewheel *The Queen of the Mississippi* at the end of August. The water was near record-low levels, and it was obvious right away as I went down the cement apron to the place where the *Queen* was docked. It was a long, low entry point, many feet below the level where Kate and I had been the year before when we bicycled along the waterway.

The arch was overhead, higher than ever from the boat. It is an illusion in many ways, reflecting the sun, casting shadows like lassoes that take in different vistas as the day passes. It is the Gateway Arch, the commemoration of the nation's journeys summed up in the travels of a ragtag group of adventurers led by two unimposing figures named Lewis and Clark.

Here is the gateway to the Louisiana Purchase, to the Pacific Northwest, to the far side of the Mississippi River. Trails converge here. Lewis and Clark did not really start here, even though their winter camp is available in a park on the Illinois side. They were not born here, and they had not lived here. They were across half the continent, on the Ohio River, by the time they reached their winter camp. The great arch stands halfway along the Mississippi River water trail, the Great River Road, and the steamboat and commercial travel routes. It is also the place where the Trail of Tears and the Underground Railroad intersect with the flow of commerce and pioneers.

Great wagon trains would leave from here to find the overland trails to the Pacific. Mountain men would bring in the skins of dead animals that had been collected as far as the Rocky Mountains. Railroads would go north and south and east and west. Steamboats vied with flatboats and were replaced by barges and towboats. At St. Louis, a great bridge was designed by James Eads, who would also construct the ironside boats of the Civil War. Many forces would converge to make this the center of all the potential that was the United States in the 1800s.

Going downstream there were large rafts of barges and some nice sections of forested shore. One barge sat on a broad sand beach, landlocked

after the river level dropped. Wing dams stood high and dry, erupting from the water like rock walls separating private sections of beach. Further downriver we passed Kaskaskia, which had been a French Colonial town, the administrative center of the British Province of Quebec, added to the state of Illinois when it was taken by Virginia Militia in 1778 by George Rogers Clark's brother, William Clark. In 1818, when Illinois became the twenty-first state, the town briefly served as the state's first capital. This is pertinent to the Mississippi River study because in 1881, flooding by the river not only destroyed most of the town, but also shifted the river to the east. The flooded river captured the last ten miles of the Kaskaskia River and made it the main Mississippi River channel. This left the former state capital on the Missouri side of the river. Legislation ensured it would stay part of Illinois, but it is west of the river and reachable only by Missouri roads. The area code is Illinois, while the zip code is Missouri.

Chester is a blufftop community that celebrates its most famous citizen, Popeye. Their other fame would have been as a major center in the castor oil trade, which made the town famous for a while. Originally this medicinal liquid was made from the oil pressed of castor beans, but the

name "castor" might have a longer history with the Mississippi River. In the north, the beaver were taken for their fur and for the hat trade, but they also provided castoreum from their glands, which was thought to increase brain power—just as wearing a beaver top hat made a person smarter. The bean also produces the toxic compound ricin. It is made today, but not in the massive quantities, and most farmers now grow soybeans and corn.

Chester is hometown of Elzie Segar, the creator of Popeye. Elzie created Wimpy, Olive Oyl, Bluto, Sweat Pea, and others as part of *Thimble Theater*. Each of these characters was based on a Chester, Illinois, citizen, including

Popeye, who appeared in the tenth year of the then-syndicated comic series. From that point on it was Popeye, the spinach-eating sailor, who went on to fame and *Thimble Theater* faded from memory. The town has an annual Popeye Festival, but unfortunately it was the weekend after I left.

I walked the streets of the quiet village and then took the city steps down the long, steep bluff. I might have breathed hard going down except it would have looked bad to the woman and her two dogs, who blazed past me jogging back up the steps.

Going downriver, there are many small towns tucked into the shore. Grand Tower was formerly named La Tour, Jenkins Landing, Cochran's Woodyard, and Evan's Landing, all of which reflect the history of this site. Early non–Native American settlers were river pilots who had been driven off by both the Spanish and the United States army dragoons.

Now the big landmark is a pipeline. As the boat approached, I at first thought it was a bridge. An amazing array of wires set up a support system for the natural gas pipeline that crosses the river.

The low water meant more than large sand bars, sand beaches, and sand bridges. It also meant quicksand. It is so easy to think of these sandy areas as places to play—great beaches for volleyball, sunbathing, and campsites—but the low level causes water beneath the surface to move

toward the lowered river level. When water moves under sand it causes the grains to roll, lose their edges and become a sink of miniature ball bearings. It is saturated sediments, but because it is sand grains, and therefore, quartz, it does not have a surface texture like mud. The sandbars are actually ledges of sand rather than solid accumulations with water behind, in front, and under them. According to records I could find, it was 1988 when the river was last this low, and in that year at least seven people died in the quicksand. Quicksand was involved in these tragedies, but at least on one occasion the tragedy included the collapse of the sandbar into the river itself.

Cape Girardeau welcomed us with a mural-lined seawall. This town is founded on the site of a trading post established in 1733 by a French soldier from Kaskaskia, Illinois, named Jean Baptiste Girardot.

It is a town with beautiful buildings and a lot of turmoil—not including the upsetting fact that the Limbaugh name is on many buildings. It was the hometown of the verbose and obnoxious radio mouth. His ancestors were more respectable attorneys and judges who earned the naming rights.

I liked the typical river brick buildings, but I was most impressed with the convoluted history that included four Union Army forts that

defended the north within this slave state. One of these was constructed under the leadership of John Wesley Powell, who would lose an arm in the conflict and go on to lead the United States Geological Survey, as well as taking the first boat expedition down the Colorado River through the Grand Canyon. I have always been inspired by him. The battle of Cape Girardeau took place April 26, 1863, and in four hours, twenty-three Union and thirty Confederate soldiers lost their lives.

The greatest tragedy recorded here is the Trail of Tears. Creeks walked along with other tribes who were moved from their homelands with little protection in the December cold. They crossed the river near what is today Trail of Tears State Park. This place has a very disturbing past, but I was inspired by the forest and trees and the best overlook on the river.

Going to the park I passed "Little Egypt," a settlement like Thebes (the next community downriver, Cairo, and Memphis from the area known as Little Egypt). Thebes did not make an impression, but I know it is the home of Captain Andy Hawkins, his wife, Parthenia, and their daughter, Magnolia, from Edna Ferber's novel *Show Boat*.

The Little Egypt portion of Illinois is a distinct region bordered by the Wabash, Ohio, and Mississippi rivers. There are a few theories about how the name arose. Some say it is a valley like the Nile Delta, and others say it was an area where people had to go for grain when the harvests in the north were poor. It is also said that the sands that developed in drought and the flood overflows were reminiscent of the Nile.

The final city before the junction of the Ohio and Mississippi rivers is Cairo, the tip of Little Egypt. Coming around the point into the Ohio River, Fort Defiance State Park was on my left. This fort was commanded by Ulysses S. Grant and has the lowest elevation within Illinois. Today, it is surrounded by levees.

Cairo was founded by the Cairo City and Canal Company in 1837 and was one of the most important cities on the rivers until the riverboat trade diminished in importance. The current population is just a shadow of the former glory—the population was over 15,000 in 1920, and is currently under 3,000.

The Ohio River doubles the size of the Mississippi with a flow that comes from Pittsburgh, Pennsylvania, through Ohio, Illinois, Kentucky, and Indiana.

Ohio River to Memphis

I HAD THE OPPORTUNITY to go up the Ohio River for forty-seven miles to Paducah, Kentucky. It was a great experience to be able to see the two rivers come together and flow side by side, mixing only gradually, the Ohio extending its length to the south the way the Amazon fresh water keeps separated from the ocean for 100 miles. At Paducah, I got to see a similar effect when the Tennessee entered the Ohio.

At Paducah, some barges come from the Mississippi to the Tennessee River and the Tombigbee Canal. The 234-mile system connects the Tennessee River near Paducah to the Black Water and Tombigbee rivers near Demopolis, Alabama. There are ten locks and dams and a 175-foot deep cut to connect the riverways. The question of cost-effective use of two billion dollars is often raised—the answer is difficult and I cannot justify it.

Paducah's position is at the confluence of the Tennessee and Ohio rivers is upstream through two Ohio River locks, #52 and #53. These will be eventually replaced by a larger, single lock and dam that has been under construction for a decade and will continue to be under construction for most of my life.

There are a number of interesting stories about Paducah, from Grant's occupation of the town for the Union Army to the original land claims that were given to William Clark, of Lewis and Clark fame. I noted one sign saying the land was bought from the Native Americans for five dollars, and along my walk I saw real estate signs for Paduke real estate—I wonder how much you can get for five dollars now. But then, the chief had no negotiation powers to work with.

Investigating the story that has been told, it is now considered to be myth. Originally, legend says there was a village called Pekin, a combined community of Chicka-

saw Indians and European-American settlers, in 1815. The waterways were attractive, and the Native Americans were friendly. Chief Paduke was said to have a wigwam low on the bluff where he welcomed travelers.

But in 1827, this idyllic setting would change. William Clark had a famous older brother, George Rogers Clark, a Revolutionary War general who fought in the far western reaches of the new nation. As a result, Clark was given a gift of land—Paducah—disregarding the fact that others actually lived here and had claimed the land. The deed passed on to William Clark, who was then the superintendent of Native American affairs for the Mississippi-Missouri River region.

The story goes that he asked the chief and his people and all the settlers to move and got no resistance. The deed was issued by the United States Supreme Court, and it is noted that it only cost five dollars to process. The chief saw the proverbial handwriting on the wall and moved. Clark surveyed the land and then named it in honor of the chief he displaced. He welcomed the original settlers to "buy" new plots. The Native Americans could not live there, but he invited Chief Paduke to come to the ribbon-cutting celebration. The irony is that Paduke died of malaria on his return to his new home. That is quite a story, and we have nothing to substantiate it other than the fact that the land was given to William Clark by his brother and he plotted a town and named it Paducah.

The second terrible event was when Ulysses S. Grant took charge in 1861. This was a major supply depot and in a "northern slave state," which meant Kentucky could continue with slavery, but did not leave the Union. Grant put Stephen Hicks in charge. The racial issue that arose in 1862 was when General Order #11 was issued, requiring Jewish residents to leave their homes. Grant was trying to break up the black market for cotton and chose the kind of answer that despots have chosen frequently over the millennia: blame it on the Jews. Fortunately, President Lincoln met with Grant and had him rescind the order. Overall, Grant seemed to be quite open and accepting, but this one issue is a stain on his record.

The Union depot was attacked by Confederate General Nathan Bedford Forrest in 1864. His raid was a temporary setback for the Union army, but short lived as Forrest immediately moved further south.

From Paducah to the Mississippi is a triangle of land known as the Jackson Purchase. It was not truly purchased, but instead taken from Chickasaw ownership by Andrew Jackson when he forced the Chickasaw to go on the Trail of Tears.

Now the city has become a place for walking and exploring. I found a great pie shop just up from the boat and walked twelve miles of city streets to find old architecture and some great stories. I had no idea that this was the home of the National Quilting Association nor that the National Quilt Museum was here. Inside the museum I met the "YoYos"—a group of elderly quilters who specialize in a circular form they call a yoyo, and it does look like one of the sides of my old childhood toy. These are incorporated into larger quilt projects and all the proceeds go to support area non-profits.

Walking further from the river brought me to Lower Town, the historical art district. I met an artist who was in his yard with his dogs. He

explained that these old homes had been in disrepair, rundown and going fast when the community, in partnership with the local banks, decided they would give any artists who would move here a small cash stake and 100% remodeling financing. Artists swept in, rescuing the buildings and giving the neighborhood a renewed vigor. The information center for the district is in an old restored Texaco gas station.

Museums are everywhere in the town—Civil War, railroad, Mississippi River—and all are worth some time, but it is the murals on the levee wall that really captured the stories, from William Clark to "Atomic City." I did not know this atomic history. It began in 1950, when Paducah was chosen to be the site for a uranium enrichment plant, which continues to supply atomic energy plants today. Yellowcake, a dense form of solid uranium, is the product of the Four Rivers Paducah Gaseous Diffusion Plant.

According to a report by the local public radio station, "The U.S. Department of Energy owns the land and leases the buildings to USEC. The entire property encompasses just under 3,500 acres. 750 of those are limited acres, protected by tight security, upon which uranium is enriched. Business goes twenty-four hours a day, 365 days a year."

Returning to the Mississippi, the next stop would be New Madrid, on the famous Boot Heel of Missouri. The Boot Heel is a geographic oddity like the Northwest Angle in Minnesota. It does not follow the convention of boundaries marked by straight lines or geographic features (rivers and coasts). The explanation from the Missouri Secretary of State website says,

> The inclusion of the "Boot Heel" in the boundaries of Missouri has been credited to John Hardeman Walker, a landowner and influential citizen of southeast Missouri. Walker was born in Tennessee in 1794 and came to the New Madrid area of the Territory of Missouri at the age of sixteen. When the New Madrid earthquakes began a year later, in December 1811, many of the area's citizens moved away. Walker, however, did not leave the area and his cattle-raising enterprise; instead he acquired more property and soon became known as the "Czar of the Valley." His extensive landholdings were located in Little Prairie, near present-day Caruthersville. This area fell under the jurisdiction of the Missouri Territory as administered from the town of New Madrid.
>
> In January 1818, the United States Congress received the first petition requesting permission for the Missouri Territory to organize a state government; other petitions were presented over the next couple of months. At that time, the southern boundary for Missouri was fixed

at 36°30'. Walker and the people of Little Prairie realized this line would place their lands some twenty-five miles south of the Missouri border. Little Prairie would be under the jurisdiction of the Arkansas territorial government, not the state government of Missouri. Walker, who preferred the area, and his holdings, to be under the protection of Missouri state laws, lobbied in Missouri and Washington, D.C., for inclusion of the "Boot Heel" within the boundaries of the state of Missouri.

And as the cliché goes, the rest is history.

What New Madrid is most famous for is the 1811 and 1812 earthquakes—three major ones and a series of aftershocks that were also serious (around a thousand, according to some articles). There were no true measures of earthquakes in those days so the estimate of force can only be inferred by scientists who look at the resulting land disturbance, and most consider that the magnitude had to be near eight on the Richter scale. What we must keep in mind is that the differences in earthquake ratings are logarithmic—that is, the jump from a six to seven rating is not the same as from seven to eight. A seven is ten times more severe than a six and an eight is ten times greater than a seven, making it 100 times greater than a six!

The three main shocks came on December 16, 1811, at 2:15 A.M., January 23, 1812, at 9:15 A.M., and February 7, 1812, at 3:45 A.M., meaning the devastation took place both in the night and in winter. For comparison, these shocks are thought to be two to three times as strong as the 1964 Alaskan earthquake and ten times the 1906 San Francisco quake.

The results from earthquakes are unnerving. Dry land was wet, wet land was dry; ruptures opened up, blocking horses and wagons; geysers of both water and sand erupted; islands disappeared; chimneys and homes toppled. There was motion and turbulence within the earth, and waves in

seemingly solid ground generated waves in the water. Blockage of the river by erosional deposition and shifting sediments created temporary dams and water flowing downstream met water being forced back upstream, creating a sense of complete chaos. People in Nashville and Louisville were panicked. Sand and water ejections reached tens of feet into the air.

A letter written by Eliza Bryan contained this terrifying account:

On the 16th of December, 1811, about two o'clock A.M., we were visited by a violent shock of an earthquake, accompanied by a very awful noise resembling loud but distant thunder, but more hoarse and vibrating, which was followed in a few minutes by the complete saturation of the atmosphere, with sulphurious [sic] vapor, causing total darkness. The screams of the affrighted inhabitants running to and fro, not knowing where to go, or what to do—the cries of the fowls and beasts of every species—the cracking of trees falling, and the roaring of the Mississippi—the current of which was retrograde for a few minutes, owing as is supposed, to an irruption [sic] in its bed— formed a scene truly horrible."

Because Tecumseh had told the tribes that he met that he would stomp his foot to awaken all the Native Americans to his cause, the earthquakes became part of the lore surrounding the War of 1812 and the Indian War within it.

The quakes all impacted the arduous journey of the first steamboat from Pittsburgh to New Orleans. The boat, named the *New Orleans*, with its owner Nicholas Roosevelt aboard, proved its ability through the earthquake-ravaged river. The captain had to sort out the new passages from old islands and create a route that had never been taken before.

Today the land feels stable but there have been over 4,000 seismic reports of earthquakes since 1974.

The river is wooded, with industry poking through the forests and interrupting the forested batture (land between the levee and the river) and the sandy shorelines until Memphis. Here the large city that denotes the beginning of the lower Mississippi is spread out from Mud Island, parkland, and a boat landing in the floodplain.

In Memphis I met Highway 61 again, the same road that runs near my home and up to the Canadian border, which is a reminder that the city contains many converging stories. Memphis was the Wall Street of the cotton economy, and the landing where we were anchored would have been in the midst of paddlewheels, cotton bales, traders, slaves, and mules. The Cotton Exchange tracked the trading of the south's most important export and because of this activity was also one of the largest slave markets. It also sold mules and has the distinction of being the world's largest mule market right up to the 1950s.

The Civil War military battles here were short and mostly on the waters of the Mississippi, where ironclad Union ships fought with cottonclad Confederate vessels. The land conflict is commemorated with a small Confederate park on the upper bluff line looking over the visitor center and Mud Island complex. The only other significant event in the Civil War

skirmishes was a rebel raid by Nathan Bedford Forrest (there is a statue of him on his horse in his namesake park). In the Civil War, he was known as a daring and successful cavalry raider and after the war he became the first Grand Wizard of the newly formed Ku Klux Klan.

This had not made a big impression in our research, but on our first visit while on the *Queen*, around 11:00 P.M., Kate heard sounds of people yelling and making noise along the river parkway and looked out to see white-robed members of the KKK marching up the sidewalk. We learned the next morning that they were in town for their National Convention. It was chilling for us to see and also disappointing. Such a disgraceful legacy.

Not far from the landing is the Lorraine Motel—now part of the Civil Rights Museum. It preserves the site where Martin Luther King, Jr., was gunned down. In my youth, the assassination of Dr. King and both Kennedys marked a terrible time of disillusionment and despair, but the words of Martin Luther King continue to spread hope, unlike the KKK.

In a sense, Memphis has had a true history of kings. Elvis Presley's home, Graceland, has become a mecca for the rockabilly King's fans. The house is toured by thousands, his accomplishments are displayed, his home is open, and his grave is there. It has become a pilgrimage site. Sun Records and Stax Records are two of the icons of music—Stax brought the sound of Otis Redding, the King of Soul, while Sun had Presley, Cash, Lewis, and Perkins, all representing the economics and vibrancy of the city. And, of course, there is a third king in Memphis musical history.

Beale Street is anchored on one end by the home of W.C. Handy, a small blue shotgun house, with appropriate signage. He is considered the father of blues. Two blocks toward the river is B.B. King's "The House of Blues" that anchors the lively street scene. And Riley—B.B. (Blues Boy) King—was truly the King of Blues.

Chapter Nine

The Lower Mississippi

MIKE

THE LOWER MISSISSIPPI is not a mirror image of the upper, and the contrasts are startling. Our choice of taking sections of river and a variety of boats whenever they were available actually aided us in a way we had not anticipated, letting us go back and forth and see the amazing contrasts found over the 2,350 miles (3,782 kilometers) of river in different seasons and conditions. We could compare the shipping channel from the Gulf of Mexico to Baton Rouge with the creek-sized flow from Itasca to Bemidji. There were locks and dams below Minneapolis to St. Louis and then levees and control structures to keep the water in the channel instead of spreading out over the natural 200-mile wide landscape that was the historic path of floodwaters.

In the far north there were extensive marshes with freshwater birds and mammals, while in the south the brackish landscape held extensive wading birds and waterfowl, nutria, and alligators. Deciduous conifers in the north are the bog-loving tamaracks, and in the south, the cypress. In the north were tributaries adding to the flow while in the south there were distributaries and bayous, removing water from the channel and disbursing it on a variety of routes to the Gulf.

Back and forth, the river was alternately tiny and huge. The contrasts were obvious in the towns and the land use. In the north we struggled to get access because of ice and snow melt not happening until May 17, while in the south we found the waters open and rising from flood events in Illinois, Iowa, and Missouri. In the north, people wanted to live beside the river, to be part of its flow. It was recreational and inspirational. In many places in the south, the levees were walls built to separate the towns and people from the water. The river was flood, poison, and danger. It was a working river.

Memphis

WE HAD HOPED to catch a ride on a paddlewheel and ended up becoming employees of the *Queen of the Mississippi* as Riverlorians, sharing our stories and perspectives with people from all over the world who had dreamed of floating on the mighty Mississippi. The *Queen* is a new boat owned by the American Cruise Line, and it divides the Mississippi up into the three navigable stretches we have outlined. People are drawn here for many reasons—plantations (think *Gone with the Wind*), New Orleans (the party and celebration city), Memphis blues, and the Civil War are four reasons. Steamboats, Mark Twain, and desire for a Huck Finn raft all contribute to the attraction of the Mississippi.

From the blues in the delta to jazz in New Orleans, to Cajun zydeco and the calliopes on the paddlewheels, there is a musical background to this region which is rich and diverse. Styles criss-cross, banjoes twang, horns, bass, and piano combine, gospel singers and Elvis impersonators all have a place on the river.

To come to Memphis and not visit Beale Street would not seem right, but there are many other great places we walked to and investigated. For example, on Mud Island is a very large three-dimensional map of the lower Mississippi, complete with cities, islands, and water. It is a work of art, an overview of the river, and a play area for young Tom Sawyers and Becky Thatchers.

From Mud Island we crossed over to the visitor center, where giant statues of B.B. King and (the King) Elvis are found (they need one of Martin Luther King, Jr., too). Then we followed the paths along the river and up to Confederate Park. Here the brief battle of New Orleans was fought. Cotton row is the street where the Cotton Museum can be found, and large mercantile buildings reflect the commerce that made this the Wall Street of the plantation era.

Danny Thomas's St. Jude's Hospital is a tremendous story of one man's dedication to making life better for thousands of children, and the Civil Rights Museum commemorates the efforts of thousands of people to ensure a life of freedom in this country.

Finally, there is a park along the river, near where the paddlewheel ties up, that has a statue of a young black man, Tom Lee, rescuing a white man from a shipwreck. In one very heroic effort, Tom Lee saved the lives of thirty-two people who were drowning after a steamboat, the *M.E. Norman*, capsized. On May 8, 1925, the ship was carrying attendees and families of the Mid-South convention of the American Society of Civil Engineers when it began listing, capsized, and sank rapidly.

Twenty-eight-year-old Lee was in his skiff. He had just returned from taking a man to Helena, Arkansas, when he saw the boat go down.

Lee went into action, despite the fact that he could not swim, taking people to the shore and returning to get more. Twenty-three people died, but they all could have perished without Tom Lee's heroism. In appreciation, the engineers raised the money to buy a home for Tom and his wife. Now an excellent set of statues commemorates this heroic feat.

Going to Vicksburg

HELENA, ARKANSAS, is the next major community along the river. This stretch of river has low forests and lots of sandbars and islands.

The White and Arkansas rivers converge here, but do not connect as they enter the Mississippi River. Both are large flows and interesting rivers, but the White is the only one I am really familiar with, having canoed the Jack's Fork, Current, and Buffalo Wild rivers that empty into the White. Near its mouth it becomes part of a National Wildlife Refuge. The refuge's website says it is one of the largest remaining bottomland hardwood forests in the Mississippi River Valley and, "during some years, up to 350,000 birds will winter in these flooded bottomland hardwood forests."

When we passed Greenville I thought of the written images in the John Barry book *Rising Tide* that describes the flood of 1927 and the terrible rise of racism as desperation brought out the worst in many people.

Floods are a natural part of the river system, but not this levee system. In normal rivers, the flow spreads out over natural floodplains depositing sand at the point where the river leaves its normal course, resulting in natural levees. Behind these levees the slower waters move laterally and often will stay wet long after the flood subsides. These are places where organic silt deposits form rich soils, the kind that supported the Nile River and Egypt over the millennia until the Aswan Dam. It is the rich soil that created the delta country between the Yazoo and the Mississippi and the richest cotton-growing district in the United States. The floods were a form of natural revitalization that supported large populations of birds, fish, turtles, gators, and other life, but levees were built to keep the water within the confines of the navigable channel. The floodplains suffered.

In 1926, a weather system stalled in the valley. Rain filled the streams and converged in the Mississippi River. In the spring of 1927, the system was still pumping water into the tributaries and the accumulated snow and ice in the north melted. In the spring it kept raining. On the "Mississippi Now" website, Princella Nowell gives some details of this picture, quoting the diary of Henry Waring Ball:

> April 8, 1927... at 12 it commenced to rain hard and I have seldom seen a more incessant and heavy downpour until the present

moment—9:00 P.M. I have observed that when the river is high it is always raining. The water is now at the top of the levee, and we have heavy showers and torrential downpours almost every day and night. The air is saturated with moisture, and the luxuriance of plant growth is extraordinary. Nell went through pouring rain to the garden club.

[April] 15. The worst Good Friday I ever saw. A night of incessant storms, wind, lightning, thunder and torrents of rain. Raining constantly all this morning, none of us slept much. A day too dark and stormy to go to church or even out of doors. Discomfort. Flowers and plants beaten to the earth, little half-drowned chickens in baskets in the kitchen, house leaking in many places. Everybody in a bad humor except Jane, the cook. River appallingly high, and levees in very precarious condition. Too dark to write, another big storm coming—noon."

Then Nowell writes, "The steady rainfall filled streams, bayous, creeks, and ditches in the Delta region and saturated the farmland. As the water rose in the Mississippi River and levees broke in other states, all indications were that 1927 would be one of the worst years for flooding." In natural levee systems the water is supposed to spread out; in human systems the idea is to keep it all in and flush it out to the Gulf of Mexico. But nature can outdo human effort. All thirty-one states in the watershed were contributing to the rising water level and as the levees were breached the flow went into towns and plantations instead of floodplains. The walls of the levees were like earthen dams that paralleled the river, and the height of the river within the levees exceeded any ground outside the river.

When leaks occurred, the water left the river and rushed down the slope, gaining speed and power. Water followed water, flows widened and endangered everything. The Greenville levees were the weak point in the system, the place where the most damage could be done. Nowell says, "The crevasse was so huge it allowed a volume of raging water that covered nearly one million acres with water ten feet deep in ten days."

Using dogs and shotguns, some of the levee foreman forced the African-Americans to stay and work while white families fled. No pay, no support, and racism became a tragic second story. Men were forced to lie in the levees—as human sandbags—and the tragedy became one of additional horror. Some were forced to unload Red Cross supplies and food, but were denied access to the food.

John Barry describes the horrible concentration-camp conditions in his book *Rising Tide*:

> Percy ordered all Greenville blacks to the levee. The camp stretched seven miles. Percy ordered that all the Red Cross work be done for free. There were too few tents, not enough food, no eating utensils or mess hall. Black men were not allowed to leave—those who tried were driven back at gunpoint by the National Guard.
>
> The food they received was inferior to what the whites got. Canned peaches came in, but were not distributed to blacks for fear it would "spoil" them. Whites kept the good Red Cross food for themselves. Giving it to the blacks, one white man explained, "would simply teach them a lot of expensive habits."

On our various journeys we watched the captains on the *Queen*, Max Tabor and Kenny Williams, maneuver our big craft in very high water and very low, in rain and wind and snow. We docked when the water was near the floodwall and at other times when it looked like the town had raised two stories. They avoided barges and ships, trees floating wildly and even, once, me in my smaller craft.

This is a highly skilled position and one that we have grown to really respect. Here are Kenny Williams's thoughts:

> I was born and raised in Alabama and it was either work as a logger, which I did for two years, or work in a cotton mill and I didn't want to do that, so I finished high school and moved into New Orleans the next day and started working on the river. I was on a boat for four days and the captain asked if I could drive, and I was seventeen and thought he was asking if I could drive a car and I said, "Yes, sir."
>
> He said, "I am going to bed" and he went to bed and I didn't know much, but I knew if I turned on every light on the boat someone would recognize me. So I turned on all the lights and everybody would say, "Come in, boat with all the lights on." I got it up and down the river okay. I decked one summer and found it was hot. Decked one winter and found it was cold and I wasn't old enough to get a license. I opened the book and thought, *I can't learn it*, but I'd already scheduled the test so I went up there. It was back in '73 and when I went in there, there were about twenty people in the Coast Guard

place. The Coast Guard man said, "All right, everybody taking the written test sit over here, everybody taking the oral test sit over here." So I sat on the written side. He would read the same questions over, read the wrong answer quick, read the next wrong answer quick, read the right answer and tap on the board, read the right answer and tap on the board. I changed one or two of them, but I passed.

Then I just kept getting upgrades and upgrades and now I can run the big ships that run up and down here. I can run on the Nile, the Amazon, and the Great Lakes. Now you have to be nineteen to start getting your license and it takes almost five years to have enough time just to sit for your license. And once you have got your license, then we can start teaching you. And it takes another two years to be able to sit up here and then another two years before we can let you go by yourself.

We fished on the Cousa and the Telepousa River in Alabama. Never crossed my mind ending up on the Mississippi. You have to work out there first. You have to learn to push the coal, the grains, the wheat, and then you advance to the chemicals, the gasolines, and the diesels. I worked for NASA a few years and pushed the fuels for the space shuttle. Then when you have done all of that, you are allowed to push the most valuable cargo out here, which are you people.

Vicksburg, Mississippi

THE TOWN OF VICKSBURG has suffered the malady of small towns everywhere, the death of a downtown. I really do hate the box stores; the downtown has fascinating old buildings and a ghostlike charm, but there is hope. Investors are working to get people living downtown, where they can walk and shop and hopefully provide the incentive for new businesses. At this point the development is mostly near the National Military Park, which is the big draw for tourist dollars, but people need to realize that the battle took place right in the downtown area and the new restaurants and opportunities can support a larger exploration of the two-month siege.

Those who do not come to the waterfront miss a lot. I love the paintings on the floodwall. The stories here are diverse, like the fact that the first bottling of Coca Cola was done in a local drugstore, Theodore Roosevelt refused to shoot a bear that was tied up and so the legend of the Teddy Bear began, Jefferson Davis lived nearby, and steamboats made this a regular port of call.

COTTON
AMERICA'S KING
GREETS
AMERICA'S PRESIDENT

The Army Corps of Engineers has a very good free museum in town that looks at the history of the river, there are museums at the old depot and the old courthouse, plus the Coca Cola Museum is on Main Street. The group that controls the fate of the river—generals and military, not paddlers and lovers of the natural river—have their imposing headquarters across from the new city hall. The old city hall is where General Grant raised the United States flag on July 4, 1863, and forever changed the July Fourth celebration for Vicksburg.

Walking around the streets, we saw the mansion where General John Pemberton had to contemplate surrender of the Confederate troops shortly after receiving a note from some of the starving men saying they would revolt if not fed. This note is an interesting object because no one knows who wrote it. Some speculate that Grant not only used the Navy and the Army, but also had a small air force of kites that would bring documents to the town—an aerial assault that might have included such documents as the letter to Pemberton. The reality is, what the note said was still true.

You can also find red markers along Main Street where gun emplacements were established to hold off the Union control of the river—an important reminder that the war was not confined to the battlefield, but rather was first fought from the center of the business district. A bed and

breakfast claims to be the mansion where Jefferson Davis made his first public presentation after being told he was president of the Confederacy. His plantation was nineteen miles away and this was his brother's place at the time. He was on his way to Montgomery, which was the Confederate capital at the time. He had famously stated, "Vicksburg is the nail head that holds the South's two halves together."

Walking among old mansions and vast live oak trees is the best way for me to enjoy the city. I also like walking the national park. The cruise arranges for buses, but I prefer to walk, to take my time and see the battlefield as the soldiers did. I find the park very sad; the loss of life and the suffering that took place here is beyond anything I would ever want to experience.

I always visit the Minnesota and Wisconsin monuments here and think of the men who served. I also revere the occasional woman masquerading as a man who came from the north to fight in this war. It was a war of humanity. Some like to say it was a war of state's rights rather than slavery, but that is only because of the Madison compromise, which made the choice of slavery up to each state for twenty years, delaying discussion of the horrid institution.

Jeffrey M. Schmitt, from the Florida Coastal School of Law, has this to say about the causes of the war:

In the decades leading up to the Civil War, the most important legal, political, and social issue of the day—the subject of slavery—provoked one of the country's first and most contentious disputes over the extraterritorial application of state law. When arguing for the rejection of southern law, northerners asserted that any forced application of the law of slavery would infringe on fundamental aspects of the sovereignty of the northern states. In response, southerners contended that, under implicit principles of federalism which commanded that southern law to be treated on equal terms, northern states were constitutionally required to apply southern law when ordinary choice of law rules so dictated. Facing this conflict between principles of state sovereignty and state equality, northern courts followed traditional legal doctrine by holding that state sovereignty must prevail.

The result of a compromise was written into the constitution: "The Migration or Importation of such Persons as any of the States now existing shall think proper to admit shall not be prohibited by the Congress prior to the Year one thousand eight hundred and eight, but a Tax or duty may be imposed on such Importation, not exceeding ten dollars for each Person." James Madison was the primary writer of this document, and he was also a slave owner. It was a way to put off the slave question, with many thinking that the slave trade would end of its own accord.

General Charles Cotesworth Pinckney told the South Carolina House of Representatives, "In short, considering all circumstances, we have made the best terms for the security of this species of property it was in our power to make. We would have made better if we could; but on the whole, I do not think them bad."

Numerous battles were fought along the river—Island Ten, Fort Jackson, Memphis, New Orleans, Port Hudson, Greenville, and Vicksburg, to name a few—but Vicksburg was key because it had steep loess bluffs that looked right down on the Mississippi. On April 16, 1876, the Mississippi River changed channels and left Vicksburg high and dry. Now we come up an artificial channel that diverts the Yazoo River. When the river broke through DeSoto Point it did what the Union army could not accomplish.

In 1863, the guns terrorized any would-be river traffic. But under Admiral Porter the Union fleet slipped by. It was a dark night for the first part of the flotilla and the city had been engaged in a party at the Balfour house, next door to General Pemberton's headquarters. The timing was perfect and the ships with all their supplies were free on the Mississippi.

In the meantime, Grant used the bayous and meanders to get around the channel and below Vicksburg, where he was successful in crossing the river and setting up a rear action where the final battles would be waged. It was the largest amphibian landing in history until World War II.

Grant's actions set a lot of parts in motion. He met Johnston's troops in Jackson and routed them, gaining the state capital. Johnston did not reorganize and retaliate, but rather he ordered Pemberton, who had been waiting for Johnston to reinforce him, to attack Grant. This action was too little, too late. The Confederates thought Grant would be slow and waiting for his supply train, but Grant chose to have the troops survive on what

they could gain from the land and the plantations. This light infantry action with a large force was not expected. Grant did not fortify Jackson, but rather moved back toward Vicksburg and engaged in two decisive battles—Champions Hill and the Black River—where Pemberton was forced to scramble back to their fortifications and hold Vicksburg as Jefferson Davis had mandated.

Grant, Sherman, and other subordinates laid siege on Vicksburg, but not before two ill-advised frontal attacks that cost the Union dearly. The siege was long and painful for the soldiers and the town. Grant's leadership won the battle and with this victory and its counterpart, Gettysburg, on the same day, the north finally began to win the war. The battlefield at Vicksburg is one of the nation's most important historical parks.

St. Francisville, Louisiana

FROM THE FERRY LANDING where we docked it was an easy walk to the town of St. Francisville. We passed through the lower wetland forests and glimpsed birds and flowers within the trees and gators in the open wetlands. Mostly it is hardwood forests, but there are some open cypress areas and the overall feeling is a true southern landscape. First the road goes through Port Sara, established in 1790—a prosperous town until it was wiped out by floods. Uphill is St. Francisville, "two miles long and two

yards wide," on top of a narrow ridge overlooking the Mississippi River. It was a Confederate town that supplied the regional plantations.

It had been the capital of the Republic of West Florida for seventy-four days. This republic bordered the Gulf of Mexico on the south and extended from, but did not include, present-day Florida west to Baton Rouge. The Louisiana Purchase put this land in question. It was not in the sale to France, and Spain attempted to retain control, but the citizens rebelled. Of course, this independence did not last long with the United States as their neighbor. To the pleasure of some and the chagrin of others it was annexed by the red, white, and blue, and the blue flag with a single white star in the middle stopped waving over the region.

Local attractions include the Button Museum, located in an old bank building, and a boutique of unique women's clothing and jewelry with a variety of miscellaneous items, including a collection of the old-time Mississippi River buttons in the old safe.

The Grace Episcopal Church and cemetery is a historic location tied to some fascinating stories. The cornerstone was laid by Confederate general Leonidas Polk, the fighting bishop, who, stories say, fought with his command and fellow generals as much as with the Union forces. The cemetery also holds the remains of federal gunboat captain John E. Hart, who died of suicide on a gunboat in the Mississippi. The tale is that he was in so much pain from wounds that he took his own life. However, he was popular with his men and they did not want to drop his body in the river. They held up a white flag and negotiated with the Confederates. The selling point was the fact that he was a Mason and so were many Confederates. The ceasefire lasted long enough to bury the captain with both Union and Confederates at the grave. Afterward the Union soldiers returned to the ship and both sides commenced fire again.

Another famous military man, General Robert Barrow, died on October 30, 2008, at the age of eighty-six and was buried in the Grace Episcopal cemetery. He was the twenty-seventh commandant of the United States Marine Corps. The *New York Times* wrote: "General Barrow combined Southern courtliness, fierce devotion to Marine tradition and courage reflected in dozens of awards. He was awarded the Navy Cross in Korea and the Army Distinguished Service Cross in Vietnam, both of which are second only to the Medal of Honor." His family was from the famous Rosedown plantation. And just to make finding the grave even more important, I had, walking with me, a retired military surgeon who served and ran with the general at the Pentagon.

Plantations abound in this area. Rosedown typifies the image of the grand southern plantation tradition. The two-story mansion sits at the head of an alley of massive live oaks. At its peak, the plantation consisted of 3,400 acres, most of which was planted in cotton. In order to maintain the production of their crops and the lifestyle to which they were accustomed, the Turnbull family kept as many as 450 slaves. Today the plantation and the remaining 371 acres is a state historic site, maintained by the State Parks of Louisiana.

The Myrtles Plantation, which dates to 1796, gets its name from the surrounding lush pink crepe myrtle trees. The house is less ostentatious than other plantations and has been converted into a bed and breakfast. The real draw today is its reputation for being haunted.

We found the Oakley Plantation most interesting because of its connection to John James Audubon, one of the most famous men of the Ohio and Mississippi River valley. His presence in St. Francisville, while short, is the basis for the Annual Audubon Pilgrimage the third week of March. Audubon was hired in 1821 by the lady of the house, Mrs. Pirrie, to tutor her daughter, Eliza. While he only spent three and a half months at Oakley, it is where he painted thirty-two birds for what would become his "Birds of America" collection.

Audubon was in an ideal place for his project, but the financial arrangement came to a halt when the daughter, a seemingly difficult child, was too sick to draw and paint, and that left Audubon with time to do his own thing. However, he was still there and wanted and needed the pay, but the woman of the house refused, saying he did not do the obligatory number of lessons. Back and forth it went. The father, a friend and ally of Audubon, was helpless in this situation, and John was terminated.

Baton Rouge

As one might imagine, in an area that was English, French, Spanish, Native American, and American, the concept of a capital is one that fluctuates. There was Louisiana Territory, the Republic of West Florida, and the state of Louisiana—each with different boundaries and, therefore, different locations for the principal palace of power. The first "capital" of French Louisiana was Mobile, in 1717. Next was Biloxi in 1720 and New Orleans in 1722.

When Louisiana became a state in 1812, the capital was New Orleans, but many people complained that the legislators were having too much fun, drinking too much, and accomplishing nothing, so it was moved to Donaldsonville in 1830. The legislators thought they would die of boredom, so they moved back to New Orleans in 1831. In 1849, the capital moved again, this time to Baton Rouge, and during the Civil War it was easily occupied by the Union Army, so Opelousas was chosen in 1862, Shreveport in 1863, and New Orleans in 1865. Its final move (we think) was back to Baton Rouge in 1880.

The Republic of Florida still has its presence in Baton Rouge: the oldest neighborhood sits in the shadow of the capitol building. This neighborhood, begun in 1803, was commissioned in 1805 when the United States purchased Louisiana Territory. The Canary Islanders who lived on ceded land moved here to stay on Spanish soil. Now it is a community of artists and creative people who decorate their property with flamingoes and maintain a Mardi Gras tradition.

The city has a waterfront walkway and museums, including the "Old Capitol," which resembles a castle and would have been one of the truly unique capitols had they not built the Huey Long skyscraper. The design of the exterior is elaborate and the interior is ornate, with a massive winding staircase encountered at the entrance. Mark Twain did not see the quaintness in the castle when he wrote the following in *Life on the Mississippi*:

> Sir Walter Scott is probably responsible for the Capitol building; for it is not conceivable that this little sham castle would ever have been built if he had not run the people mad, a couple of generations ago, with his medieval romances. The South has not yet recovered from the debilitating influence of his books. Admiration of his fantastic heroes and their grotesque "chivalry" doings and romantic juvenilities still survives here, in an atmosphere in which is already perceptible

Mike Link & Kate Crowley   217

the wholesome and practical nineteenth-century smell of cotton factories and locomotives; and traces of its inflated language and other windy humbuggeries survive along with it. It is pathetic enough, that a whitewashed castle, with turrets and things—materials all un-genuine within and without, pretending to be what they are not—should ever have been built in this otherwise honorable place; but it is much more pathetic to see this architectural falsehood undergoing restoration and perpetuation in our day, when it would have been so easy to let dynamite finish what a charitable fire began, and then de-vote this restoration-money to the building of something genuine.

This new Huey Long building not only replaced a castle, but it gave the state the tallest capitol building in the United States. From the statue on the capitol grounds to memorials and plaques, there is no missing Huey Long. He is buried beneath the statue and the Huey Long immor-talized in the statute stares right at the capital, a reminder that he still has expectations.

The "Kingfish" was governor, senator, and Louisiana's favorite son; unless you happened to hate him, as did his assassin. In the capitol build-ing there is a case in the hallway behind the elevators with news clippings and artifacts from the assassi-nation. In addition, there are patches in the wall and a bullet in one of the marble columns. What one learns standing there is that the assassin was not the assassin. There is even some historical questioning of why he was there. The official Huey Long website states,

"On September 8 [1935], Huey was in the state capitol in Baton Rouge for a special session of the Louisiana leg-islature, pushing through a number of bills including a

measure to gerrymander opponent Judge Benjamin Pavy out of his job. According to the generally accepted version of events, Pavy's son-in-law, Dr. Carl Weiss, approached Huey in a corridor and shot him at close range in the abdomen. Huey's bodyguards immediately opened fired on Weiss as Huey ran to safety."

In the confined marble hall, Huey's body guards opened up, probably firing every bullet they had, and the ricochets were everywhere, including a bullet that struck the governor. Robert Travis Scott, writing for the *Times Picayune* in 2010, had this to say about the conflicting stories:

> Of all the versions of the shooting, [State Police Captain Don] Moreau's is perhaps the simplest and the least inspired by specula-tion. The seven witnesses closest to Long at the fateful moment de-scribed essentially the same chain of events and they stuck with their testimony for the rest of their lives, Moreau said.
>
> He said the accidental ricochet theory is weak because in reality the bullets would not have tended to bounce around in that hallway and, if they did, they most likely would have struck one of the many other people standing nearby. No one was hit but Long, Weiss, and possibly one of the guards who had his wristwatch knocked off.
>
> The version of the story—in which Weiss quickly stepped forward and got off one or maybe two shots before being knocked backward and shot by the bodyguards—is the one that has the most evidence to support it, Moreau said.

Huey was unlike any governor and had more power and influence in the state than anyone else in Louisiana's history. He was best known as a "share the wealth man," a populist who could put the screws to big business and anyone who got in his way. One story we heard—and we're not sure if it is true—was about a bridge that Huey wanted built and wanted the railroads to pay for it.

The Huey P. Long Bridge, which we passed under (actually, we went under two bridges with the same name), was built in 1935 as a can-tilevered railroad bridge at river mile 109—New Orleans. This was the first bridge over the Mississippi in Louisiana and now it has three lanes of U.S. 90 on each side of the central tracks. The railroad had been using a train ferry across this location for a number of years. According to the page

for Huey Long on the website "Louisiana Social Studies," "Long's critics accused him of being a dictator but he did introduce important reforms. This included the provision of free school textbooks, free night school courses for adult illiterates and increased expenditure on the state university." I mention this quote because it makes the story seem more feasible.

The story says one of Long's representatives told the railroad that they needed to build the bridge and pay for it. Of course, the railroad said no, they were happy with their ferry. They were informed that that was fine, but the new tax for the ferry would equal the cost of the new bridge and by the way—add car lanes on each side of the track.

The second bridge, this one in Baton Rouge, which is referred to as the Long Bridge as well as the Huey Long Bridge, marks the spot where ocean-going ships can no longer travel up the Mississippi River. Some say it was the Kingfisher's intention to keep Baton Rouge as the end of the ports connecting to the saltwater Gulf.

A visit to the new capitol should include a visit to the upper deck, where one can enjoy long views of the city and the river. It will show how close one is to the chemical industries that exert pressure on the legislature. The old capitol is now a museum of Baton Rouge, as well as state politics.

As for the city itself, Mark Twain had a colorful description in his *Life on the Mississippi*:

> Baton Rouge was clothed in flowers, like a bride—no, much more so; like a greenhouse. For we were in the absolute South now—no modifications, no compromises, no halfway measures. The Magnolia trees in the Capitol grounds were lovely and fragrant, with their dense rich foliage and huge snow-ball blossoms. The scent of the flower is very sweet, but you want distance on it, because it is so powerful. They are not good bedroom blossoms—they might suffocate one in his sleep. We were certainly in the South at last; for here the sugar region begins, and the plantations—vast green levels, with sugar-mill and negro quarters clustered together in the middle distance—were in view. And there was a tropical sun overhead and a tropical swelter in the air.

> And at this point, also, begins the pilot's paradise: a wide river hence to New Orleans, abundance of water from shore to shore, and no bars, snags, sawyers, or wrecks in his road.

New Orleans

THERE IS A DIFFERENT feeling down here for a northern paddler. Cancer Alley is more than a conglomeration of chemical plants and petroleum refineries. It is also a traffic jam of oceanic vessels and barges competing for the channel and docks. The shoreline along this stretch is marked by towers, chimneys, storage tanks, pipes, and futuristic conglomerations of metal.

Coming into New Orleans relieves this feeling and takes you to the most exotic point in the United States. There are few cities that truly make an individual statement, and New Orleans is at the beginning of the line. The Jazz National Park, Louis Armstrong Park, and Jean Lafitte National Park surround the city and capture some of the history and complexity that allows thousands of writers to capture different images of the Big Easy and still be correct.

Jimmy Delery is a tall, lanky, middle-aged man with a walrus moustache and a taciturn visage. We met him through a friend, as he was recommended as someone who knew the area well and could help us learn more. We first walked through the French Quarter with Jimmy, and he told us this version of New Orleans history:

A long time ago the Indians, because of the bounty, the water, and land, and the trees and all, settled here. Then along come the Spanish explorers and they realize that this is a beautiful great river. And they take note of it and explore the rest of North America. And the French get antsy. They realize this is the place to settle and control the Mississippi. With that the French settled and we began a colony here in 1718. And Iberville and Bienville, who were brothers, put together this colony. My family got here at that time.

My ancestor was a captain in the regiment and my family settled here. My last name is Delery, but the real name of our family is Chauvin. Three brothers came here and they took on different names. [...] We were part of the French settlement of Louisiana. Over time it went French, Spanish and back to French and then Napoleon, I think, needed a little cash. So he sold Louisiana to a very smart colonist, Thomas Jefferson.

And Jefferson realized the value of Louisiana. [...] Thomas Jefferson had a vision of how great the Mississippi would be. The original colony that was here was more of a fort. The real development of Louisiana was when the Germans came with their families and settled in. [...] The Irish came over as indentured servants. The Africans came over and worked the plantations. The Irish did a lot of building here and worked on the docks. [...] Then we had what we would call our Italian immigration, but truth be told they weren't Italians, they were Sicilians.

As each culture came in, it not only brought people from all over the world, but they brought something that would make New Orleans unique. Here in New Orleans we have this great soup called gumbo and it's all these different parts that come together and form a single soup.

Today we refer to the gumbo of our cultures. It is these differences that really makes us unique.

The Mississippi River . . . was the super highway for commerce. The 1984 World's Fair [in New Orleans] had the theme, "The World of Rivers—Fresh Waters as a Source of Life." That has been critical for us. [...] And really for us the critical thing is where that freshwater meets the salt water and we refer to that as brackish water and that is really the womb of our seafood

Later, he drove us through the Ninth Ward, where we could see houses still marked by the post-Katrina clean-up committee, and around to where the sand within the levee, near Lake Pontchartrain, became a

weak spot that enlarged as water moved through and created a pathway for oncoming tidal surges.

Bob Thomas, a professor at Loyola University who runs the Center for Environmental Communications, spent a day taking us to Bayou La-Lutre, wetlands that are being saved around the city, and then to a wonderful dinner location outside all the downtown areas where we could sum up the day and the conditions we were seeing. Here are Bob's comments:

> I have lived here since 1977. I grew up in central Louisiana from eighth grade through high school and then I went to undergraduate school at the University of Southwest Louisiana.
>
> We are doing a lot of things. One of the things I am working on now is with the U.S. Business Council For Sustainable Development, moderating their water synergy project. That is an initiative to get industry to come together up and down the river to talk about water; how they use it, what their constraints are, and what they think about water-related projects, which would include everything that they take out of the river to disposal of water back into the wetlands we are trying to save. You know industry uses a lot of water, so anything we can do to make them conserve is important to us down here.

It is also important to see how they deal with the Mississippi River water because we know the Mississippi has a lot of chemicals in it, a lot of nutrients and herbicides, and these guys have to deal with it.

One of the things we are very concerned about down here is the coastal erosion issue that we have to deal with to serve the nation as the nation wants to be served. About forty percent of the fisheries of the continental United States come out of our waters because of our coastal wetlands. And then about thirty percent of the oil and gas that comes into the country comes in through Louisiana, whether it is from offshore drilling or imported through our LOOP program off-shore, where they unload the big ships.

The LOOP, LLC website describes its primary business as "... offloading foreign crude oil from tankers, and storing and distributing the inventory via connecting pipelines to refineries throughout the Gulf Coast and Midwest. LOOP is also the storage and terminal facility for the Mars and Endymion pipeline systems and their supply of offshore domestic crude oil."

Bob continued,

We need to rebuild our coast so that it stabilizes. Everything we design to protect the coastline of Louisiana for our interests and the national interest involve the hydraulics of that river. At the same time, there is

no long-term plan and no management plan for the Mississippi River System. What we are concerned about is that the Texas Water Board has a plan that is still on their books where they would like to take water out of the Mississippi and take it to Lubbock, Texas. Las Vegas, Nevada, is trying to negotiate a way to shunt water out of the Missouri River because they are building a major metropolis in the Mojave Desert. And they desperately need water, so they want to import it from the Missouri which keeps flooding, right? So they are telling people, "We'll solve your problem. We try to help you by taking the water that floods you." And if that happens, that will be less water coming down to New Orleans.

Georgia is in court right now to try and get access to land between their border and the Tennessee River so they can tap the Tennessee. Their aquifer is getting low. The Tennessee flows to the Mississippi.

When you are a large city and do not have water, a long way becomes doable. All of our plans are based on the hydrology of that river as it exists today.

If you put the five ports in Louisiana together, they are the largest port for tonnage in the United States. The calculation is that if that river closes down, as it did during Katrina, every day that it is closed it costs the American economy $300,000,000. As a matter of national security, you have to be concerned about these things."

Below New Orleans

TRAVELING SOUTH with Jimmy Delery, we went to Venice and the marina at the end of the road. When we got to the end of the road, we had to drive through water that was flowing over the road and up to the base of the car—it seemed like tangible evidence of global warming. Jimmy wanted us to see the fishing community here at the end of the land. We parked the car and watched yellow-crowned night herons in the trees. Beyond the natural forest curtain were stacks of oil industry, in stark contrast. Then to top off all the things we saw and felt, we found a group of pelicans coated in oil and standing among many

of their dead brethren. This was a terrible scene and through our photos and Jimmy's contacts we got the word to the Louisiana Fish and Wildlife and the local Fox News channel called and interviewed us, while others asked to use my photographs. Sometimes publicity is the best incentive for action.

At Woodland Plantation we met the owner, Foster Creppel, who shared his insights on what is going on in the sinking land and rising waters of the southern peninsula, which is now trapped between two levees and open water instead of miles and acres of marsh.

I have been here sixteen years. The plantation was built in 1834, Spirit Hall was built in 1873, and we moved it here in October of 1998. Moved it fourteen miles. In the 1790s, William Johnson and George Bradish, who built Woodland later, originally built Magnolia Plantation and they were the first American river pilots. They worked for Juan Ronquillo, a Spanish river pilot who controlled the deep delta. He was the predecessor to today's bar pilots and the pilots who move boats up and down the river.

When they built Magnolia Plantation they also built two two-story brick slave quarters that were situated right where this building [Spirit Hall] is now. They were in cahoots with Jean LaFitte. Jean LaFitte would steal people's schooners and boats and steal their slaves off shore and then bring them up Grand Bayou—a shortcut to the gulf. So he would bring the slaves up Grand Bayou and store them at these brick slave quarters, so if you believe in spirits, the spirits of those people could still have been haunting these grounds. They had a lot of people in those and it was terribly hot.

So we took this building that was created for healing, spirituality, and forgiveness and moved it fourteen miles and put it over the grounds that had seen all this pain and suffering and now everyone is welcome to enjoy spirits [it is a bar]. That's why we named this building Spirits Hall.

Mainly we are a twenty-five-room country inn that caters to fishermen from all over the country. We are open twenty-four-seven by reservation only. My dad was a fighter pilot in the Air Force so I grew up living a lot of different places, but he's from Crown Point, Lafitte area which is right across the marsh.

On my father's side I am from the bayous; on my mother's side from New Orleans. I don't think I will live anywhere else . . .

We asked him when he talked about the fishing being good whether he was talking about the river or the marsh. He answered,

I am talking the marsh, the estuary of southeast Louisiana. The Mississippi Delta, which is rapidly washing away. It's a terrible thing. I used to be really optimistic that we could do something. I used to go to all the meetings and I thought, *we can do something about this*. Sixteen years ago I thought that, ten years ago I thought that. I am not as optimistic anymore.

I guess when I started really thinking, *we're not really going to be able to do this*, was two years ago [2011] when we had the highest river stage we've had in some seventy years. I went to a meeting where they were all getting together . . . and I talked to these guys and we did not have one diversion or one siphon open. They had them all closed down. And I'm like, we are getting together to talk about spending these hundreds of millions of dollars for wetland restoration but we're not using the ones we have in existence. I don't know why we are all getting together as this group and talking about wetlands restoration, blah, blah, blah . . . The oil companies were there financing the meeting, the Corps of Engineers was not there and I was surprised when we have these meetings . . . why we don't have the Corps of Engineers, because they are a very important part of these conversations. I am thinking we are not really serious about these issues if we cannot bring the oil and gas and the Corps and the oyster fishermen together to talk about these things.

First of all, we cut all the cypress swamps, so that was not good, but we did that 100-plus years ago and those were swampy areas and the river used to have swamps. Some people who do not like diversions and siphons say it will kill the marsh. Well, it will kill the saltwater marsh, but there used to be swamps there. The swamps used to catch all the freshwater and all the nitrogen and phosphates and then it became saltwater and brackish on the outside. But we have not had swamps now for eighty years, they are all gone. So now when we reintroduce freshwater, we are introducing it to saltwater. Yes, it is not going to do a very good job restoring those, but it will in time, we have to be patient, reintroduce swamps. We need bogs and swamps and cypress.

Then we built the levee in 1928, then extractive companies came in and we dredged and drilled and then we dredged the oyster and clam reefs and we destroyed it. People say, "Foster, it's going to take a long time. It took thousands of years for this delta to form and to build." And I say, yes, it took thousands of years to build and we have destroyed it in about a hundred. Now to think we are going to build diversions and siphons and wetland projects and they are going to turn it around in five years is not being realistic.

The delta is a very dynamic living system. The whole Mississippi River Delta, the whole river system is. It is moving and changing all the time, but the delta especially is constantly moving and building and changing and moving and changing and we can't make it static. That's not how it builds. It's got to be a bit wild and untamed and free and we have to live above that. I tell people all the time that the only way we are going to do it is to raise our highways, raise our houses, and lower our levees. Build spillways and diversions. Yes, do some dredging. I think it is good that we take some sediment from the river and put it in to the marsh in different places, but make sure we put them in the right places and that we also introduce freshwater.

But the year I am talking about, not a drop of freshwater was diverted. During the highest river stages we have had in seventy years, we could have inundated the marshes.

One of my good fishing guides I was talking to the other day wrote an article online and said these diversions are not good for his fishing holes. And I said, "When you get to your fishing holes, are you running a natural bayou?" And he said, "No—I am running over land." I said, "Exactly, everything you are running over used to be land and you tell us when we try to restore this that we are taking away your best fishing holes. Every place you are fishing used to be marsh or it was swamp. They had freshwater bayous and saltwater bayous and we do not have these anymore."

Can we restore it when they say no? And the oyster fishermen don't want us to reintroduce freshwater, and the alligator guys over here are collecting the eggs and they are afraid the high water is going to kill all their eggs. And I am thinking, alligators have been living here millions of years. Way before we even walked the planet, alligators were dealing with freshwater and high rivers and losing a few eggs. We're not going to destroy the alligators.

We asked whether anyone said why they did not open any diversions. He said,

> Yeah—they said they were going to get sued by the oyster fishermen on the west bank and alligator egg collectors on the east bank.
>
> If we are going to get serious about wetland restoration, it is not going to be easy and a lot of people are not going to like it. And it is going to do some damage to some oyster reefs, it's going to make some folks' best fishing holes non-fishable.
>
> I remember as a kid, my grandfather lived in Crown Point and it's right where Bayou des FamNes [sic] runs into Bayou Barataria. Bayou Barataria was a freshwater bayou from the Mississippi River—dumped into the northern part of Barataria—and they had huge oyster reefs on the southern side of Barataria Bay and it had a different smell. It was that black water. It was freshwater. You've got bass living in it, you've got mink and otter and muskrat and you've got gar and crappie and all these fish that need fresh water and we had a lot more ducks. I asked my grandfather why we had all these big oak trees and palmetto here and he said that's because we have two freshwater bayous here. And I realized that that smell is going away. We have no more freshwater bayous out there.

When asked how he was affected by Katrina and Isaac, Creppel said,

Well, with Katrina, the storm came from the north and northeast and missed us to the east. If we ever have a storm as large as Katrina follow the Isaac path, we are all in trouble. It crossed the front levees on both sides of the river here. In Katrina, the small back levee helped us. We had only two inches in the big house and a foot of water in Spirits Hall. The water did not build up. With Isaac, the storm tracked south and west. It pushed all the water across the back level and we had fourteen inches here. The problem with that is there is nowhere to go—it came down some, but only as large as the levee would allow. We should have gates on the levees to allow the water to drain. Now it is all trapped.

Down here, you are either going to be flooded by freshwater or you are going to be flooded by saltwater. Which do you want to be flooded by? We built those levees to keep that river from flooding and keeping the water in the channel, but now that the river is not flooding, what are we getting flooded by? Saltwater, by hurricanes, and I think the better choice is freshwater. Saltwater will kill the whole delta.

I draw maps all the time, and I saw—look, the Atchafalaya is the first distributary. Then you have the Bayou Tache River, then Bayou Lafourch, then Bayou Terrebonne, then Barataria and on and on, all freshwater distributaries. Rivers are built by tributaries and big tributaries build big rivers. Well, deltas are built by distributaries. If you have no more distributaries, you have no more deltas."

Heading south, it became apparent that we were on the remnant of a peninsula. Where there was once marshland extending to our visual horizons, there were now two levees. It is an eerie concept. Some of this was reflected in our conversation with the only cattleman remaining below New Orleans. We met Earl Armstrong, Jr., a man who graduated from high school in 1962. He has a fascinating history in the lower river. Standing on the levee, Earl, in his straw summer cowboy hat and t-shirt, talked about his life on the river and his relationship with the Mississippi. He said, "We're in Boothville," on Grand Bay, north of Venice "right now, but I am originally from Pilot Town and moved up to Boothville in 1974. I went to school at Pilot Town up to the eighth grade and I went to school and boarded at Holy Cross High School in New Orleans. I been down here ever since. I'm the last [cattle rancher] down on the mouth of the Mississippi River."

He used to have a cousin who ranched down in the area, too, but now he is the last to graze cattle in this southern outpost.

Earl continued, "Southwest pass is the shipping channel and they're still using that channel." A large Westfal-Larsen boat come by as we talked. "This ship came in from southwest pass and the Gulf. It comes as far as Pilot Town and a pilot gets on and takes it from Pilot Town to New Orleans. The Bar Pilot will get off up here and the river pilot will take over."

We were curious about what life would be like growing up in a town that had no access to other communities except by boat. Earl told us,

> It was some of the best years of my life. I got married in '64 and I had two girls and a boy at Pilot Town who went to school there, also, and when we moved up here we had another boy and a girl. I've got three girls and two boys. One of the boys is a river pilot. The other boy does what I did: raise cattle, go fishing and trawling and whatever it takes to make a living. All of my girls are school teachers. One is a teacher here, another at Port Sulfur, and another at Folsom. I was never much at school and all my kids end up being school teachers.
>
> The first hurricane that I encountered was in 1957, Hurricane Flossy. I was thirteen years old. Hurricane Flossy was one of the first ones to start working on the marshes at the mouth of the river. I was always told a 1947 hurricane was a bad one, but they wasn't named then.
>
> This place started going down in the late '30s. We started losing land. Things started switching around. And I have been able to watch it ever since and it is not a very good thing to watch.
>
> I got married in 1964 and built a house at Pilot Town. In '65, Hurricane Betsy came, which I rode out in a Lafitte skiff. I broke loose in the night and they picked me at ten o'clock the next morning in the trees. I was still in the boat. They were well made. My brother-in-law was also in a boat, but he never broke loose.
>
> In 1969, Hurricane Camille hit on August the seventeenth and it blew harder than anything anybody has ever seen. Even harder than Katrina. We rode it out at the pilot station at Pilot Town. My wife fussed at me about getting in the boat—"promise me you won't get in the boat"—cause I'd sent them all upriver. I said, "I won't." So I was in my house and it started to go down. We had boardwalks down there then and we left my house because we knew it was getting ready to go. A tornado took the one next to mine, that my father had a good chance to see. I

felt my house shake and crack and he said he could see the next house to mine just go up in the air and into the river. We walked about a quarter of a mile to get to the pilot station. Nobody got hurt or anything, but it was a tough storm . . . The wind velocity was right at 200 or better. We got those velocities from ships and tugs that were anchored in the river. Some of their wind gauges broke at 200 miles per hour.

[Pilot Town] is just south of Cubits Gap. It's an island in a sense . . . A boat was just like a car we use here now. If you had to go to Venice to get something, you jumped in your boat and went to Venice . . . But it is one of the best places I have ever . . . I would go back to Pilot Town right now. It was a great place to raise children. Everybody looked after everybody's kids. If they saw them doing something they weren't supposed to do, they'd fuss 'em just like we would. It was one big family and lots of good people.

After Katrina, the town stopped functioning as it had historically and primarily is just for pilots now.

"This is what they call Yellow Cotton Bay," Earl said as he looked to the water to the west, only a short distance from the river. "You go out a little further and you got Bay Jack and then the Gulf, but everything in one now. It's hard to tell where the bayous were, where the bays were. Everything is breaking up into one big bay."

Earl continued, "I had a bad deal with my cattle for Katrina. I had cattle on islands down at the mouth of the river. I lost 1,800 head. Those bulls right there," he said, pointing at the pasture behind his home, "I lost ninety of those. Look, I lost, but so did everybody else . . . The people you see now are those that have enough nerve to try it again. I'm not planning on going anywhere. Someone asked me what it would take for me to leave. I said, 'When there is no more mud, that is when I will have to leave.'"

Jimmy Delery got us to the river pilot headquarters along this stretch of land, where we met Jeffery Robicheaux. "I'm one of the river pilots, one of the bar pilots," he told us. We were standing on his boat in the Mississippi River. "Right now we are beside Venice, Louisiana. This is eleven and a half miles above Head of Passes on the right-descending bank, which is the west bank . . . thirty-one and a half miles above the Gulf of Mexico."

Kate asked how he ended up being a river pilot, and we were told,

I started out wanting to be a pilot, specifically a bar pilot, when I was about sixteen years old. I'm thirty-six now. My family does have a history on the water, although they were not in the pilots. I grew up deck handing and captaining on some family charter fishing boats that went out of Empire, Louisiana. So we spent some time anchored at the mouth of the river.

Usually at the end of the day fishing I would see the ships coming in and out of the mouth of the river. My family members knew some guys that were pilots and I met some more guys that were pilots and I asked questions and decided to pursue it.

The progression from being a deck hand on a charter boat to where I am now . . . I found out there were some maritime academies in the country and I pursued my secondary degree at Texas A&M–Galveston. I have a degree in marine transportation. Upon graduating I had a third mate's license for any gross tons upon oceans. I took a couple jobs on small boats here in the Gulf of Mexico—oil field boats, and then running crew boats in the river. In fact, running these boats for the bar pilots, which is how I got to know all these guys.

When I felt like the "meet and greet" was done I went to work on my license on ships. I took a couple jobs on different types of ships and when I became eligible to be a pilot—eligibility requirements are that you have to be a resident here and have a full year at sea on a ship and a four-year degree—I started applying and five years and five applications later and one failed attempt in an election and after Hurricane Katrina I got enough votes to be allowed into the apprenticeship program. I was an apprentice with the guys who came in with me for two and a half years. I became a pilot in 2008.

Pilots, the short answer is that we get on a ship and bring them into the river that we are familiar with and they are presumably unfamiliar with. To go into more depth, we're required to go on board. . . . There is a system in place that requires pilots to go on ships. Any vessel that is registered in another country or any vessel that is over 100 gross tons that is coming from another country has to hire a state-commissioned pilot. We have licenses from [the] Coast Guard, federal licenses, but we also serve under the Commission of the Governor of Louisiana to serve as his agent. Bar pilots, specifically, we go out when a ship is going inbound. We go out to that ship on one of these [he pointed to one of their boats], pull up beside the ship, climb up a rope ladder, and then go in to the wheelhouse and have an exchange of information with the

captain. He tells us about his ship and we tell him about our river and traffic conditions, current conditions, and what not. At that point we serve as an advisor to him and his crew to move his vessel safely through this channel. That entails giving direct commands to whoever is steering the ship (giving courses, giving direct rudder commands to maneuver that ship), dictating the speed of that ship so that we do not damage any other vessels working in the area or create bad traffic situations with other vessels moving around.

We also handle the communications between the vessel we are on and the other vessels in the area. Most of these ships coming here, their first language is not English. [The people on the ships] could be Indians, or Greeks, or Chinese, or [from the] Philippines; they don't speak full English and most of the guys who run small boats in the area don't speak proper English, either. We're basically the translator to make sure that everybody out here can coexist safely and do what they are trying to do. We're handling radio communications, as well as giving directions to steer the ship.

When asked what advice he would give to people like us, canoeing the river or navigating it in small crafts, Robicheaux told us,

I would say be very alert, be very aware of what's happening ahead and astern of you. By the time someone on a ship sees you, more than likely it is too late for them to do much. Ships a thousand feet long piloting about 100 feet above the water . . . by the time he sees a canoer, he can't slow it down a lot. Be very aware of your surroundings. Be ready for anything. Try to stay as far away from the middle, as close to the bank as possible. Try to make yourself visible.

More advice to people coming down the river? Get a weather radio, try to stay in front of that. Also get a VHF radio with a charger. Find out what VHF channel is used in each area you are in and if you see something coming upriver and you are not sure, you can call them and say, "I am in a canoe. I am at this mile in the river and I just want to make you aware that I am on the river."

The thing that makes me most nervous is if I am moving a ship and it gets foggy. If it is already foggy when we get on a ship, we don't bring it in. But if it sets in all of a sudden, me and the ship I am on are okay with the fog, but it is everyone else. All this technology is great, but it makes people more bold, more brave than they would have been. So, I'm out here on a ship in the fog and what makes me uncomfortable is that I am looking at the radar, and that's my eyes, and I see a vessel in the middle of the channel coming in the opposite direction. So we immediately try to make radio contact and they don't answer and they don't answer, so I slow the ship down and try again and they don't answer so I try a different channel on VHF and they don't answer. Now I am slowing down some more. I can't see them. I am assuming they have radar, but I have no way of knowing if they know how to use it or what scale they are on because I am running and I can see three miles ahead of me. And experience has told me that these guys in recreational boats are running on a quarter of a mile scale, so I see them three miles away so I have time to react and they are coming at me [at] fifteen to twenty knots. You cover a mile, at twenty knots, in a minute and a half. If we are coming at each other and I am doing ten and they are doing twenty—that's thirty and now you are talking seconds. I do not know what direction they are going, especially if they are in the middle, so I have to wait until the very last minute to make a maneuver to miss them. If I commit to altering the course of that ship that's 700, 800, 900 feet long, once I commit to going one direction, if I want to change it takes a long time to stop my momentum. I hope they follow the rules of the road and go right.

We regularly steer these big ships around small boats.

Atchafalaya

WE CONSIDER THE Mississippi River along Cancer Alley—140 miles of refineries and chemical plants—to be a shipping canal, and the real river
would be the Atchafalaya if they did not have a control structure at the
junction with the Mississippi and Red rivers that regulates the natural
flow down the Atchafalaya distributary. We managed to get on the
Atchafalaya, the big cypress-laden distributary, with Audubon biologist
Karen Westphal. As we traveled, she spoke about the area, explaining
what we were seeing.

We are in an area of the Atchafalaya spillway called Old River, so we
are in the southern part of the Atchafalaya basin where the cypress
trees are still fairly healthy. Most of southern Louisiana was built as
Mississippi River Delta and with the river being straightjacketed now
by the levees, the bank overflow that would nourish these wetlands is
absent so the land is continuing to subside like it naturally would but
you do not have the fresh sediment coming in to replace it. Therefore
there are a lot of projects we are working on to try to mimic what nature would have done on its own. The Atchafalaya River has also been
straightjacketed by this spillway that manages, if you can call it managed, mainly for flood control and the byproduct is damage to environmental health. In many ways, they are drowning it. For cypress to
germinate the mud has to be exposed to air, and that seldom happens.

It's doing what a normal distributary should do—it's filling in the
upper areas and the eddies, you know, and the bottomland hardwoods
and then the cypress trees should be spreading out south as the delta
builds. It's doing what it should even though the people do not like it.
But the water is being kept too high. You see very few young cypress
trees because it does not dry up enough for them to germinate, and if
they do germinate, it stays too high for them to survive. You see the
saplings that do come up get covered with water for two months or
more and that is too much for them to survive. All of these trees you see
out here are a second growth and the cypress trees you will see are almost all the same age—about eighty years old with just a few older ones.

Most every place you see those flags, you see trails marked to
crawfish traps. The spillway precludes permanent dwellings so people have adapted by bringing in houseboats. Some are camps and
some are permanent houses.

Now I work for National Audubon, but my background for many, many years was as a research assistant with Louisiana State University as a coastal scientist working on land change and habitat change and how plants affect land change. That was my expertise. Dr. Paul Kemp brought me in to be project support for the other projects Audubon is doing.

The Disappearing Delta

DAVID RINGER OF THE National Audubon Society described the work they are doing in the lower river while we looked at a large aerial map of the delta region at Barataria Reserve. He pointed at the red areas that had been land, historically, but now were gone, saying,

> ... they are open water now because the river here [the main channel] has been cut off from the delta by levees, so the water and the sediment can no longer come out into these wetlands. So they are gradually sinking into the Gulf of Mexico and one of our big priorities is to install gate-like structures in these levees that at certain times of the year would be opened to let both water and sediment into the historic delta. So these areas of open water could grow again. Here at the end of the Atchafalaya we can actually see little deltas forming and we want to see that all along the coast.

When I first came to the delta in the 1960s it was a sea of vegetation, and water was distant or dispersed in the marshes. It was a rich environment, one that can no longer be found. The issues are well-known: offshore oil, pipelines, cuts in the bays and bayous, intrusion of saltwater, disappearing land, more violent climatic conditions, less protection for the land from the historic landforms, spills, dead zones, nutrients washing off the fields up north, the shipment of more of these chemicals back to the northern fields from the Louisiana chemical factories, erosion, floods, control structures, and a disregard for the natural river system.

Yet the river continues to intrigue even as the moose disappear in the north and the gar in the south. There is still a wonderful diversity that begs to be discovered and there is still hope that we can move forward for the future instead of immediate profit, that we can care about the Cajun way of life that is disappearing as the land washes out from beneath their feet and homes, that we can provide the proper habitat for seafood and remove the chemicals that make their ingestion questionable. As I write this there are articles about freshwater diversions and a battle between abuse and preservation, but at least there is a dialogue now that includes restoration.

This is the Mississippi that we discovered. We care. We want the river to run free, the Atchafalaya to gain new growth of forests, and deltas to come back. The challenge is for people along this Minnesota-to-Gulf of Mexico water route and the citizens of thirty-one states who send their waters to gather in the Great River to reach a level of understanding that will motivate them to care and to act.

Afterword

Bicycling from Iowa to Brainerd on the Mississippi River Trail

MIKE

Oᴜʀ ᴏʀɪɢɪɴᴀʟ ᴘʟᴀɴ was to bike the river down one side and up the other, but our drive had shown us how dangerous the roads could be and also how isolated from the river we would be because of the levees and the distances the roads traveled from the river itself. We biked in St. Louis and followed the bike routes in New Orleans, but putting the rest of the route together even with Mississippi River Trail (MRT) maps was not appealing. The MRT is an effort to establish the very routes we were looking for, and they chose the closest and best roads available. As the years go by new trail options are being developed and the full ride might be just what we are looking for in the future.

Many people have ridden and will ride these trails (mostly roads), but for us the dedicated trail is our preference and even when we decided to just concentrate on the Iowa border to the Mississippi headwaters, there were sections I did not like and many parts Kate would not ride. Being in our late sixties, we make those difficult choices.

I consulted the Minnesota Department of Transportation (MNDot) website and maps and the book *Bicycling Guide to the Mississippi River Trail*, by Bob Robinson. My riding was limited to two-day stretches because of injuries to my upper and lower spine and an aneurysm. The aneurysm and occipital neurology were new ailments, in addition to the seven ruptured disks, and affected my ride and plans. I found two days was good, but the second night and next day were required for my recovery.

Because of the injuries to both the vertebrates in my neck and those in my lower spine, I have switched to a Rans recumbent bike, and I am delighted. The recumbent helped support my lower back, kept me from putting weight on my injured elbows and ulnar nerve, and meant that I

would not be straining my injured neck. I still had issues, but this reduced the total impact of my pedaling.

Someday, the southern states will discover the value of a bike route that is a real trail and use the levees as they have done in the area of Vacherie and New Orleans, Louisiana, and then we will have a real trail, but until then I will call this the Mississippi River Route—not Trail.

What follows are my notes from our ride, as well as a "grade" we assigned to each section of trail. If you want to explore the river as we did, these might help you with your planning. Here are my criteria for grading the sections (you will see there are a variety of ways to make a pleasant ride).

Safety and surface: A nice, paved, separate bike path gets the highest grade, but when the road is busy and there is no paved, wide shoulder, the grade is the lowest.

Visual enjoyment: Can I see the river? That is very important. If not, is there a lot to enjoy—barns, landscape, birds? If I am just watching the traffic and reading billboards, the rating is the lowest.

Services: Is there food, air for your tires, stores, towns spaced so that they can enhance the experience? Are there nice places to eat, are there unique shops and places you want to stop and visit?

Signage: Is the route well marked? Are you sure you are where you want to be?

Iowa Border to LaCrescent, Minnesota
C

THE ROAD SURFACE was new, making the ride nice and smooth. The shoulders are not paved, but traffic is relatively light and we found lots of views of the river, including some excellent lookouts to view the islands, marsh, and backwaters and observe waterfowl. The refuge along the Root River was also excellent for bird watching, with yellow-headed blackbirds and Great egrets. As you can see from this first note, we are not out for speed or just exercise. The bike is a means to slow travel with lots of observing.

La Crescent, Minnesota, to Onalaska, Wisconsin
B

HIGHWAY 16 IS a very busy road with a good shoulder into La Crescent, but not an enjoyable ride. Crossing over to La Crosse on Highway 14 is a good option with a wide lane to ride, and the views of the Mississippi are the best! There's a good, safe lane over one of the river's best bridges (for beauty, this ranks with the Stone Arch in Minneapolis and the John James Audubon in Louisiana). After the bridge, the best path is to drop back down to the river on the walkway next to the bridge, hit the riverfront trail, and go through the parks until you come to the La Crosse city bike trail system at the La Crosse River and take this trail to the Great River bike trail. Hard

to beat! We encountered a section flooded out, which might happen often in the spring. Great birds, backwaters, and biking, although the trail does come out to the road (River Valley Drive) and requires some path riding next to the road, and in this section the surface needs a lot of work.

Onalaska through Trempealeau Wildlife Refuge, Wisconsin
A

THE SURFACE GETS a little soft when it is wet, but otherwise the crushed lime works great and this trail is worth an extra ride just to enjoy the wildlife and the scenery. We were there in May and I could not think of any better time. There were lots of flowering shrubs (with minimal leaves that allowed us to see the waves of migrating birds), good views of sunning turtles, and the flooded backwaters of the Black River. In Trempealeau, there are a variety of wonderful places to eat, from Mrs. Sippy's, where I had an amazing burger, to the Trempealeau Hotel, with its walnut burgers.

The trail then goes behind Perrot State Park and enters the refuge. There is good bird watching here, and prairie as well as ponds. Note that there is a charge for riding on this trail, and I consider it a great investment to maintain such an excellent ride. At this time, the Minnesota roads were under construction, but overall it is a road ride with some good views of the river, but too much traffic when forced to get on to the main road.

Trempealeau Wildlife Refuge to Alma, Wisconsin
C–

AFTER THE GREAT TRAIL through the refuge, it is hard to be on a very busy highway (Highway 35) sucking fumes, dodging the bodies of the small birds that have been killed by vehicles, and having to look through on-coming traffic to see the river. The small river towns save this stretch and it is worth getting off your bike to learn about what these wonderful communities have to offer. The shoulder is wide, making this much safer than routes like the stretch between Marquette and Effigy Mounds National Monument. There are good views of the river and riding south it would be more enjoyable and the rating would go up. I also enjoyed the barns we passed, and at Alma the lock, dam, and Army Corps area are all interesting.

Alma to Nelson, Wisconsin
D

THE SAME AS THE previous section except there are no river views, wildlife is tough to see, and the road is busy. The only reward is at the end of the ride, when we arrived at the Nelson Creamery. This is not like my granddad's creamery visits. We get more than a jar of heavy cream—this is a cheese market with a wonderful assortment, plus a wine store, plus an

excellent restaurant! The Nelson-Trevino Bottoms between Nelson and Wabasha are along one of the best road crossings, with many pull-outs, lots of wildlife and plant life—this section would be a "B"—only downgraded because of the traffic and the bridge crossing.

Wabasha, Minnesota to Frontenac Landing, Minnesota
B

I CHANGED THE ROUTE here, riding through the streets and roads of Wabasha as long as possible. Near the river, Wabasha is a very nice city and the National Eagle Center makes it a prize destination. Going through town is really pleasant, then there is a short stretch on Highway 61 between Grant Boulevard and First Street in Reads Landing where you must be on a very fast and busy road, but the shoulder is very wide and feels safe. This is a short but quiet ride along the river, and at Eighth Avenue you can find Reads Landing Brewery, which I found to be an excellent place to find refreshment Cars need gasoline, and riders need personal refreshment, which is much more enjoyable, though you must use moderation if you're going to get back on your bike.

At this point we had to take Highway 61. It has a good shoulder most of the way. Some of it needs some repair, but we were treated to some of

the best views of the river and Lake Pepin that we could find. A word of caution: Lake Pepin is known for its winds and waves—those winds come across the lake and smack the rider along this section. It is still worth it.

In Lake City, we followed the river and left the main highway. It is very safe and goes by a park, marina, and homes—an excellent ride. Outside of Lake City we again encountered the lake and winds, but the city is located centrally on the lake and offers lots of good options for food and shelter.

The road veers away from the river as it continues on to Frontenac—some signs say Frontenac Landing. This is the least pleasant section of the ride. If you have time and energy Frontenac Park is great. I have camped, hiked, and taught bird classes in this park.

Frontenac Landing to Red Wing, Minnesota
D+

THE SCENERY IS NICE because of the bluffs, but there are no real river views until the end. The road is busy but does have a nice wide shoulder. There is a round barn, a golf course, and a prison—hardly the things that will entice anyone to ride this section. It is just a necessary stretch to get from Pepin to Red Wing. At the end is one of the most picturesque communities on the river. Barn Bluff is a landmark and has been for centuries of explorers and river men. It was even an enticement to Henry David Thoreau.

Downtown Red Wing has classic brick buildings, and eventually travelers will get to the old Red Wing Pottery building. I miss this pottery and remember traveling here with my parents when they would come down to buy dishes—none of which were saved. The city has great places to eat, shop (including bike shops), and places to stay. Red Wing is a treat and keeps the section from getting a lower grade.

Red Wing to Hastings
C (kind of)

THERE ARE TWO CHOICES. Highways 61 and 316, the normal driving route, gets an "F." No river, no scenery, no interesting communities, too much traffic, too little bike lane.

But County Road 18, which I chose, I much prefer. First, I have to say that when I left Red Wing I began on the Cannon River Trail—a nice safe trail, outstanding views of the river, good birds, interesting in every way—an "A" section, except there is no way to get on Highway 61 once you get to the Cannon River bridge except to walk up the grassy road grade. Why? Someday, someone will figure this out.

Then there is an "F" section on Highway 61—ugh! Terrible. There is some nice scenery in the bottom wet area, but four speeding lanes feel too dangerous. So turn on County Road 18, but get to your lowest gear for the toughest hill of the ride: up, around the corner, up around the corner, still up and still around the corner. *Puff, puff,* actually it is more like gasping for breath, and then after a short flat ride it is down, even steeper—I would not want to be coming from the north. I saved my brakes as best I could, but worked hard to keep my bike at thirty miles per hour.

Below the hill, it was flat land for most of the way. No Mississippi views or any river views at all until I got to the Vermilion River on County Road 54. Good farmland, low traffic, and a nice shoulder to ride on. I was going well until the road department got the great idea of putting oversized rumble strips or treads in the lane where I would ride. They did not put them on the edge, but in the middle, reducing my choices to riding on the edge of the lane or the edge of the dirt, and I chose the lane. In some places the strips ran off to the dirt, showing that drivers were occasionally distracted, and of course I was trapped by these. A perfectly safe route became an unsafe one.

Before Hastings I came to a bike trail and this wonderful trail took me downtown and near the river.

Hastings to South St. Paul
F

IF I WERE CHARLIE BROWN I would just write, "Good grief!" I know they have no choices here, but crossing over the bridge on the sidewalk is an adventure and I had the issue of construction, which continued up the large hill and the fast, congested highway. This route is a mess. They try to get bikers off, but going off to the right then the left and the left and the left and then right in a near-square is not very satisfying. Where is the river?

Nowhere near. I ended up on a road that winter had nearly demolished, Point Douglas Road, where there was a lot of traffic, no shoulder, and lots of curves. I was so intent on the road that I missed the MRT sign—if there was one—for the turn and continued north through shopping centers and onto a nice bike trail that simply stopped and I had to retrace my route.

The turn I missed went to the west and not to the river but away from the freeways. It was an okay ride but part was without blacktop, a lot was without shoulders or a bike lane, and overall it was long and not satisfying. This section needs a lot of help.

Battle Creek Park to North Minneapolis Industrial Area
A

THESE ARE THE TWIN CITIES' biking paths at their best. We are really lucky to have Minneapolis and St. Paul, which rank in the top tier of bike-friendly cities. It is because of the Grand Round in Minneapolis and the river and pathways throughout St. Paul that we could really enjoy "trails" and relax. In fact, that is the challenge of getting through this system—relaxing.

It is so pleasant to see people biking, rollerblading, walking. There are families, pets, and seniors all sharing the commons, all relishing the communal ownership of sun and space. This is the way cities should be; it is the

essence of what the country should be. For me, this is the greatest wealth: the parks, the natural landscape, the public shared and nature-owned land. With riverboats docked at Harriet Island, the Science Museum leading to the city of St. Paul, Crosby Farm Park, Hidden Falls, Fort Snelling, Minnehaha Falls, Mississippi Gorge, St. Anthony Falls, the Stone Arch Bridge, Mill Ruins and the Mill City Museum, Nicollet Island, and Boom Island, all tied together in the Mississippi River National River and Recreation Area, there is so much to see and so many people to avoid that you cannot go fast.

We crossed and recrossed the river, checked out the monuments to the victims of the I-35W bridge collapse, observed the locks and dam, dreamed about the once-mighty St. Anthony Falls—the only true water-falls on the river—and the industry and cities it spawned. There is history here, from Zebulon Pike to General Mills, and a dynamic city with options for a cold drink, a warm sandwich, and relaxation. Yes, we made it, but it was not a section we were anxious to leave behind. That's why we have covered it multiple times on both sides and even diverted to go around the lakes and follow Minnehaha Creek.

North Minneapolis Industrial Area to North Mississippi Regional Park
F

WHEN THE TRAIL ENDS at a railroad track just before the most industrial area of the urban city, I had to move out among commercial vehicles on roads with very little room between parked cars and large vehicles. In addition, the roads are in terrible shape and as I moved north I found traffic eventually being reduced but the road surface not improving. This is one of the connections that you just have to suffer through.

North Mississippi Regional Park to Champlin
B

THE REGIONAL PARK hugs the Mississippi and sits between it and Interstate 94. There are trails, playgrounds and parking areas that make this accessible. From here the trail goes along the river, under the freeway, and up to Coon Rapids Dam Regional Park. All these are "A" trails. The route then follows quiet neighborhood roads on a separate paved trail for a long time and ends up on the roads themselves until it swoops down under the

Champlin/Anoka bridge. There are lots of river views and a very peaceful travel route. It will behoove the biker to watch at the many driveway exits. There are a lot of records of people colliding with bikes as they exit.

Champlin to Dayton
C–

THIS IS A COUNTRY road ride. The good news is that there is little traffic, but the bad news is the road lacks good bike lanes or shoulders. There is one park where you can pull in and see the river before Dayton, a nice boat landing where the Crow River meets the Mississippi in Dayton, and some interesting buildings, as well as some nice farms south of the town. It is an okay rural road, but not a ride you would specifically choose.

Dayton to Elk River
D

FROM DAYTON THE ROAD has some nice looks at the river, and then it is a matter of complex roads in a growing area of development in Otsego. I lost the MRT signs so I continued on Highway 42 to Elk River, where a sign greeted me as I crossed the river and pointed me to the right when I wanted the left. I should have been on the west side of the river on County Road 39, but I did not want to go backwards to find a way.

My choice was to ride through the old downtown, which was much more interesting than the boring developments of mass-produced stores along Highway 169. I road down Main Street and slipped up again—I should have gotten on Highways 30 and 14, but I kept looking for the MRT signs and did not get any help.

Highway 10 to Big Lake/Monticello
F

My BLUNDERS LED to Highway 10. There is nothing good to say about this fast, four-lane road, except: stay off it.

Monticello to St. Cloud
C

FOR THIS STRETCH, I took Highway 75. This is a good road, but lacks views of the river after going through the old downtown of Monticello. One thing about these bike rides is the fact that the old downtowns tend to be on the older roads and not the freeways. It leads to interesting buildings, but also the depressing fact that we have abandoned these town sites to the easily replicated chains that ground like invasive species along freeway entrances. Too bad; these were nice towns when I lived here in the sixties.

The road runs between I-94 and a snowmobile trail that could be great if converted to a bike trail. I could not see the river, just a nuclear

plant near Monticello and the stacks of a power plant near Becker. The old buildings in Clearwater are still standing, but I had to imagine what we might have seen here in the past.

Just north of Clearwater you can pick up a bike path, but don't get your hopes up—it ends within a mile. Later, we crossed over I-94, and this is where we had to be really careful of off ramps and on ramps, turn lanes and merge lanes—I do not like this at all. After the freeway, we came in to St. Augusta, and then needed to go back under the freeway. This is a busy section, but short.

St. Cloud
B

HIDDEN BEHIND THE McDonald's and the apartments on the far southern edge of St. Cloud is a bike path from River Bluffs Regional Park that leads to the Beaver Islands. It is forested with some excellent views of the islands, river, and dam. The trail ends at the University Avenue Bridge. In the Munsinger Gardens is a trail that allows good views of the river and the plants. We stayed on the campus side. This being my alma mater, I had to find a few of the surviving old buildings to remind me of when I was a student. The ride through campus and the streets past old, fortress-like mansions is quiet and pleasant—at least when school is out—and

leads to a pathway that will get the biker under the very busy Division Street Bridge. The problem is that after passing the bridge, the Inn, and the convention center, we found ourselves outside a parking lot with a sign that said BIKE TRAIL ENDS, and our only alternative to continue was to carry our bikes up a set of stairs. At least there was a good view of the river and the First Street Bridge.

We took advantage of the downtown for lunch and I continued on—Kate, still adverse to non-trail riding, went back to the car. From this point on I traveled Fifth Avenue North, which is right next to the river and is excellent except for the condition of the road—watch for potholes and cracks. At the end of this section, I went up by the hospital and then got on Sixth Avenue North, which is a busy street, and was pleased to find a bike trail beside Ninth Avenue North which allowed me to make good, safe time until I came back to the river and chose to take County Highway 1/River Avenue North.

Sartell to Little Falls
C+

THIS STRETCH OF HIGHWAY 1 is a pleasant ride (even though I got my only flat along this stretch). In Sartell, the road is off the busy routes and gives excellent views of the dam, the river, the wood products industry, and the reservoir. It

also goes past some residential homes before heading to the country. The ride in the country is very nice and the road was not busy on the day I rode. Some parts of the road did lack a nice riding lane and I was forced to be on the edge of the driving lane, which marks this down. I could have used the MRT signs, too. The Great River Road signs work, but they can cross the river when you do not want and the intersections always give me pause.

The Blanchard Dam is nearby and can be accessed by a paved section of the Soo Line Trail, which crosses a high bridge and gives excellent observation points. This is the tallest head of all the dams on the Mississippi, at forty-seven feet. Above the dam, the reservoir reaches to the town of Sartell and is visible from many places on the road.

There is a long stretch where you do not see the river, but the countryside is fascinating. For example, the little community of North Prairie is only composed of a church, a farm, and a handful of homes!

Along the way are small creeks, including the one that

served as Zebulon Pike's winter camp. The road eventually leads to the Weyerhaeuser Museum and Charles Lindbergh State Park, which protects the childhood home of the great aviator and the story of his father's political exploits. It is nicely wooded and contains picnic grounds and campsites.

Little Falls to Camp Ripley
B–

IT IS A LITTLE HARD to find the right route out of Little Falls, but eventually I found Grouse Road, just north of Highway 10. There are few glimpses of the river, but the ride seems to sample the best of rural countryside and has some really nice woods to blend with the country feeling. It is an easy ride—not much traffic on my ride and a good shoulder to follow.

Camp Ripley to Brainerd
F

STARTING ON HIGHWAY 115 the road is narrow, there is no good shoulder, and at the bridge all the lanes are not only squeezed, but a railroad track goes through the road. After the cemetery, I found a small road to follow for a mile or more before going on to Highway 371. Getting across the road was the first travail, then riding on a wide shoulder was not enough to offset the speed of the vehicles, the number of trucks, and the lack of scenery. There was no sign of the Mississippi, and I felt like I was on a freeway. Then Kate caught up with me and informed me that the road entrance said "no bicycles." I checked three sources plus the book and they all used this road. I know there is no alternative unless you pedal even further from the river to get on another less-than-perfect road, which means to me there is no MRT here. It would be better to just say that than lead people to a poor experience like this.

Paul Bunyan Trail
A–

THIS WONDERFUL BIKE PATH parallels the road in many places, but it is safe and has the beauty of Chippewa National Forest to add to your pleasure. However, it does not have the Mississippi River to view even though it is provided as an alternative section on the MRT. What I should have done was take this from Crow Wing State Park north, but I did not realize the southern section was complete. This is what I meant when I said the route will continually improve. I took the trail from Brainerd to Bemidji State

Park. This 112-mile section has connections to many small towns on route to Bemidji; the primary route along the river has too much traffic and too much busy road riding for my taste.

At Walker I saw Leech Lake, the source of the Mississippi according to Zebulon Pike. This is the closest point to a river experience along the

way. The trail runs along Lake Bemidji, which is included in the Mississippi River, and crosses the outlet on the way to Bemidji State Park. This outlet is just a little way from the northern-most point of the Mississippi.

The "–" in the grade is only because of the lack of river time, otherwise this is an "A+" trail.

Bemidji to Itasca
C–

BE PREPARED TO TAKE small roads and have limited views of the river. The roads do not follow the river, so the riding is primarily country views with a few crossings. Just be sure not to miss any turns. Overall, these roads are in good shape and if riding them during the week, traffic is down. I would not ride on a weekend (including Friday). At Itasca, an excellent bike trail can take you to the end of the lake. If you want to make sure you did the whole river, you can ride up to Elk Lake, where Glazier tried to put the source. It is a fitting ending to the ride.

Bibliography

Books

Anfinson, John. *The River We Have Wrought*, Minneapolis, Minnesota: University of Minnesota Press, 2003.

Barry, John. *Rising Tide*, New York: Simon and Schuster, 1997.

Brinkley, Douglas. *The Great Deluge*, New York: Harper Perennial, 2006.

Brown, Alton. *Feasting on Asphalt*, New York: Stewart, Tabori & Chang, 2010.

Childs, Marquis. *Mighty Mississippi*, New York: Ticknor and Fields, 1982.

Daniel and Bock. *Island No. 10*, Tuscaloosa, Alabama: The University of Alabama Press, 1996.

Dufrene, Dennis. *Civil War Baton Rouge, Port Hudson and Bayou Sara: Capturing the Mississippi*, Charleston, South Carolina: History Press, 2012.

Havighurst, Walter. *Voices on the River*, Edison, New Jersey: Castle Books, 1964.

Jacobsen, Rowan. *Shadows on the Gulf*, New York: Bloomsbury, 2011.

McPhee, John. *The Control of Nature*, New York: Farrar, Straus and Giroux, 1989.

Merrick, George. *Old Times on the Upper Mississippi*, Minneapolis, Minnesota: University of Minnesota Press, 2001.

Sansing, Callon, and Smith. *Natchez: An Illustrated History*, Natchez, Missouri: Plantation Publishing, 1992.

Schneider, Paul. *Old Man River*, New York: Henry Holt and Company, 2013.

Sims, Barbara. *The Next Elvis*, Baton Rouge, Louisiana: Louisiana State University Press, 2014.

Tidwell, Mike. *Bayou Farewell*, New York: Random House, 2010.

Twain, Mark. *Life on the Mississippi*, New York: Penguin Group, 1961.

Young, Biloine. *River of Conflict, River of Dreams*, St. Paul, Minnesota: Pogo Press, 2004.

Websites

Mississippi River Trail. www.mississippirivertrail.org

Friends of the Mississippi River. www.fmr.org

Gulf Restoration Network. www.healthygulf.org

NASA Earth Observatory. earthobservatory.nasa.gov

Mississippi National River and Recreation Area. www.nps.gov/miss/riverfacts.htm

Great River Road. experiencemississippiriver.com

Mississippi State Water Trail. www.dnr.state.mn.us/watertrails/mississippiriver-/index.html

American Rivers. www.americanrivers.org/rivers/fun/america-runs-on-the-mississippi-river/